MW01074777

Mabon

The Ultimate Guide to Autumn Equinox and How It's Celebrated in Wicca, Druidry, and Paganism

Your Free Gift (only available for a limited time)

Thanks for getting this book! If you want to learn more about various spirituality topics, then join Mari Silva's community and get a free guided meditation MP3 for awakening your third eye. This guided meditation mp3 is designed to open and strengthen ones third eye so you can experience a higher state of consciousness. Simply visit the link below the image to get started.

https://spiritualityspot.com/meditation

Table of Contents

Introduction

Mabon, also commonly known as the autumnal equinox, is a sacred time of celebration for many Pagans and Wiccans. It is a time to celebrate the harvest season and pay tribute to the deities associated with the harvest. This is not just a time of celebration but also a sacred time of shifting balance when day and night are equal in length. This makes the season-changing festival even more significant to many modern pagans and Wiccans because it is a time to reflect on the blessings received. Thus, many rituals and spells are performed throughout the festival, each deeply connecting to the autumnal equinox.

Whether you have just developed an interest in esoteric religions or are a newly practicing Wiccan or pagan, this book is perfect as an interesting yet uncomplicated guide to help you celebrate Mabon as a Pagan and make the most out of the autumnal equinox through your rituals and spellwork. You will have to understand various aspects to celebrate this festival with full fervor and make use of this sacred time for important spells.

To fully understand Mabon and its rituals, you must learn about the lore and various mythical stories associated with each event. This includes not only the story of the Celtic god Mabon but also short stories and myths about other deities associated with this holiday. Then, this book introduces you to the different fruits, plants, and herbs associated with Mabon. Fruits and plants play a significant role in this festival because they signify the harvest season and its many benefits.

To make the festival even more festive, decorate your home with the special homemade decorations we have added to the book. You will find easy step-by-step instructions for some really great and unusual harvest goodies to get you into celebration mode.

Your Mabon altar is also a very special part of the festival, and an altar has a sacred value. So, to celebrate the autumnal equinox properly, you will have to learn how to set up the Mabon altar. It is also essential for the many rituals and ceremonies that surround Mabon. However, there is no need to look elsewhere; in this book, you will find a detailed list of traditional rituals and ceremonies performed on the autumnal equinox.

Finally, there is a whole chapter dedicated to Mabon food. So, if you are a food lover, this is what you will want to read. It is full of Mabon recipes with signature ingredients of the autumnal equinox. Plus, the chapter will also tell you how to bless your food with the magical properties of Mabon.

The time of the autumnal equinox is full of magic, and the high spiritual energy should be manifested to its full extent. To properly celebrate the festival, it is important that you properly understand every aspect of the equinox.

Chapter 1: Introduction to Mabon

Wiccans and many other pagan groups celebrate eight Sabbats yearly, which are significant festivals. The Sabbats are considered great opportunities to get in touch with the unity of the universe. They serve as a reminder that the Earth and the extraterrestrial, or the physical and the spiritual realms, are intrinsically linked. The sunset of the day of the Sabbat marks the beginning of the festival, and the sunset of the following day marks its end. Magic and rituals are carried out at night.

The Sabbats are divided into two groups, greater Sabbats and lesser Sabbats. The former group originates from western European, or ancient Celtic traditions, while the latter group marks the transitions of the seasons. As you can tell, the Sabbats alternate between earth-centered and solar-based events, creating what we know as the Wiccan Wheel of the Year. Each Sabbat is associated with a certain deity, who is honored by pagans on that day. The festivals are also an opportunity to celebrate the cyclical essence of nature, conduct healing rituals and magic, and use spiritual powers. People who live in pagan communities get together to celebrate the Sabbats and engage in communal rituals.

The four seasonal, or lesser Sabbats, comprise two Equinoxes, Spring and Fall, and two Solstices, Summer and Winter. Besides celebrating the changing weather, harvesting seasons, and singular qualities each festival symbolizes, the Sabbats also acknowledge the change in darkness and light. The Spring and Fall Equinoxes are the two points of balance or stability; this is the time of year when the length of day and night are the same. On the other hand, the Solstices are transitional periods, where light shifts to greater darkness or darkness shifts to great light.

1 November marks the start of the Wheel of the Year. Yule (Winter Solstice) starts on or around the 21st of December and is the first festival of the year. Imbolc, the second festival, falls during the earlier days of February and marks the signs of fading winter and the onset of spring. Ostara, which is the Spring Equinox, takes place in March, followed by Beltane, which falls in early May.

Litha, who is also known as Midsummer, is the Summer Solstice. This is the longest day of the year and takes place any day between the 19th and 23rd of June. Lughnasadh, the sixth festival, falls on 1 August. This Sabbat is followed by Mabon, our topic of interest throughout this book, which falls any day from 21 - 24 September. Mabon celebrates the Fall Equinox and the abundant harvest. Samhain, the last Sabbat of the year, falls on 31 October 31. Alternatively known as All Hallows' Eve (Halloween), this festival is the most popular pagan holiday. All the dates we just mentioned are in accordance with the Northern Hemisphere.

Now that you understand what the Sabbats are and where Mabon falls on the Wheel of the Year, the rest of this chapter will dive into this celebration's historical and cultural origins. You will learn everything you need to know about Mabon's ancient and current traditions. We will also explore the various perspectives of the holiday. Finally, you will come across the most significant Mabon symbols, colors, incenses, herbs, plants, animals, and stones.

The Origins of Mabon

As we have said, Mabon, one of the eight Wiccan Sabbats, celebrates the Autumnal Equinox. Since this is a seasonal festival and dates differ between the hemispheres, the Northern hemisphere celebrates it around September 23, while in the south, it falls around March 20. In the north, the festival of Ostara is celebrated on this day. Ostara is the Spring Equinox (Mabon's counterpart). Besides marking the Autumn Equinox, Mabon is associated with the mid-harvest or second harvesting season.

Mabon falls on a day when everything is in perfect balance. On the equinox, day and night are exactly the same lengths, creating a sense of balance and equilibrium. This stability is not only limited to the daytime and nighttime. It is merely a symbol of the duality of nature, which can be seen in the masculine and feminine, dark and light, inner and outer, and the physical and spiritual, all falling into balance. Not only is this state of idealism and perfection celebrated, but the transition to the time when the darkness overshadows the light is also acknowledged. Mabon is a reminder that the cyclical nature of the world is slowly approaching a stage of completion. From that moment on, the days will shorten as the nights become longer. The weather will grow cooler as the sun's vigor declines. Green wanes as golds, browns, oranges, and reds take over the scenery.

This Sabbat is named after Mabon, the God of Welsh mythology. Mabon is also called the "Child of Light" and is the son of the Earth Mother Goddess (Modron). The festival was not named until the 1970s as a part of the reconstructed paganism movement. You may be surprised to learn that there is little evidence regarding the celebration of Mabon in Celtic regions, and the celebration of the Fall Equinox is not exclusive to Wiccan or pagan practices. The harvest is an important time for many civilizations, and it was the time of year that brought an abundance of food—the reason there was so much celebration. The Bavarians have long held harvest festivals filled with feasting and joyful celebration. The chances are that you have come across the word Oktoberfest or heard of this festival before.

Other cultures, including those in the USA, celebrate the second harvest, viewing it as a time to give thanks. This makes sense because Mabon is when farmers check on their summer crops and animals to see if they will be able to sustain their families throughout the harsh winter. This is a time when people express their gratitude for what they had in life—food, animals, and future wellbeing. The original US holiday fell on October 3, which is more logical in an agricultural sense because the harvest season is practically over by the time November arrives.

Apple picking is often incorporated into this festival. The picking of the apples provides food for the celebration and is also symbolic of reaping what was sown. Dedications are given to the gods and goddesses as the apples are picked and eaten. Many rituals are performed at this time of the year, most associated with balance and harmony. You can set up an altar at this time of year or decorate it with the suits of the harvest. Considering that it is deeply associated with concepts of gratitude and giving thanks, the celebration is best observed with family and friends.

Since Mabon is at harvest time, it is a good time for evaluating one's own efforts in terms of harvest, crops, and animals. It is the time of year when you "reap what you sow" in all aspects of life. In Mabon, people look back at the goals and hopes they set for the year at Imbolc and Ostara. They take a moment to evaluate their current situation, how their plans have unfolded, and whether their aspirations have manifested. Mabon is the perfect time to complete plans and projects that you've been putting off. It is also a reminder that you must let go of what no longer serves you as you prepare for the coming of winter, which is essentially a period of deep reflection.

Mabon Then

Unlike the names of other Sabbats, which are linguistically tied to other ancient pagan or Christian holidays, Mabon's name cannot be traced back to any single significant event in the past. However, as we have mentioned, celebrating the Fall Equinox and harvesting season has been considered a legitimate holiday by numerous cultures. The English festival, the Harvest Festival, was always held during the early autumn but never tied to a specific date. People played games to celebrate the holiday and conducted rituals to honor the harvest. They made corn dollies, had parades, and held feasts. Even though not everyone who celebrated was necessarily pagan, Harvest Festival is essentially pagan, considering that it celebrated the cyclical nature of the universe and is linked to agricultural cycles.

In early agricultural societies, it was of utmost importance to develop close relationships with one's neighbors. Besides being hospitable, people wanted to ensure that their neighbors would help them out whenever they could not sustain their families at the end of the harvesting season. This is why communal feasts were held, especially in rural areas, where people celebrated their harvest with their neighbors. Feasting and drinking with bread, cattle, wine, and beer were involved.

Mabon Now

Most Wiccans and pagans still view this time as a period to foster communal ties, relationships, and kinship. Many people associate pagan Pride Day with Mabon, where food is one of the most important factors in the festivities. This symbolizes bountiful harvests and encourages people to share the abundance with those who are less fortunate.

If you wish to celebrate Mabon, the best thing that you can do is express your gratitude and thankfulness and reflect on all the good aspects of your life. Honor the balance, as well as the darkness and light within. Even if you are the only one who celebrates Mabon in your community, you can explain the concept of the festival to your friends and family and invite them over for a feast. Modern-day celebrations include seasonal foods and drinks, such as tomatoes, eggplants, grapes, grains, carrots, peppers, potatoes, pumpkins, and onions. If you think about it, it is a lot like thanksgiving.

The Various Perspectives on Mabon

Ancient Britain and Ireland

As we have explained above, Fall Equinox has been celebrated for centuries by numerous civilizations. In ancient Britain, the solstices and equinoxes were highly significant occasions for those who came long before the Celts, Saxons, and the Romans. Stonehenge is a prime example of the structures built to measure time, particularly the equinoxes.

Stonehenge.
https://unsplash.com/photos/aJj87xsnVQA

These celebrations cover all of the Celtic nations. In Ireland, cairns were built to measure the falling of the equinoxes, much like Stonehenge, and they are positioned to capture sunlight in a specific way at a specific time of the year. These cairns were designed in a way that the rising equinox sun slipped right into a long corridor, lighting up a back stone. Astronomical symbols were engraved on the back stone.

Christianity

The Christian church did not take to other deities being revered, and they disagreed with most pagan rituals. This meant that the solstices and equinoxes were disliked, but instead of outlawing them, they changed the festival to align with Christian values. That is why many Christian celebrations fall on the same days as Pagan celebrations, such as Christmas and Michaelmas.

Native American Tribes

Various ancient Native American groups built stone structures that are still intact to this day. A modern-day researcher named one of these structures Calendar One because of the way it can be used to determine the occurrences of the Summer Solstice, as well as the Fall and Spring Equinoxes. This structure, which can be found in Vermont, is built on land that is around 20 acres and looks like a natural amphitheater.

The Southern Californian Native American Tribe Chumash conducted sun ceremonies during Hutash, or September, in celebration of the Fall Equinox. This festival was celebrated after collecting, processing, and storing the year's harvest. According to Chumash's myth, we are all the children of the sun, which shows how significant this celebration was. At that time of the year, the tribe pondered concepts of unity, the harshness of the winter, and the cyclical nature of life that is birth, death, and ultimately, rebirth.

Ancient Celts and Druids

The ancient Druids also had their own take on the festival. During the Fall Equinox, the Celts at the time made figures out of wicker that represented the spirit of vegetation so they could "sacrifice" them. Many suggest that this practice led to the belief that the Druids used to conduct human sacrifices. Although no one actually witnessed a human sacrifice at any Druid ritual, many people shared this belief, particularly because the rumor was given credence by Julius Caesar.

France

The calendar was permanently changed when the French revolution spread across France in the late 1700s. The fall equinox became New Year, and Vendemaire (the grape harvest) became the first month. However, they allotted 3o days to each month and left five of six extra days when the end-of-year celebrations took place.

The Mayans

You are probably familiar with the popular ancient Mayan pyramid in Chichén Itzá. The number three has always been powerful, and triangles were placed together to create pyramids, multiplying the number. You will also find many Mayan pyramids that reflect the light in a certain way during the equinoxes or solstices. This served as a guide during important times of the year.

Mayan pyramid Chichén Itzá.
https://pixabay.com/es/photos/chich%c3%a9n-itz%c3%a1-m%c3%a9xico-pir%c3%a1mide-1025099/

Neo-paganism, as you already know, is a movement aimed at the revival of ancient pagan traditions, spirituality, and religion. Wicca is the most popular of these religions and combines ancient Celtic ideas, beliefs, practices, and modern magic rituals and ceremonies. The difference between Neo-pagan and Abrahamic religions is that the former view time as cyclical. In contrast, the latter perceive time as linear, starting with God's first creation and ending at a decided time.

To an extent, these two beliefs have coexisted peacefully for millennia. That was until December 21 (or 23) 2012 arrived. Based on ancient Mayan calculations, this date would mark the end of their calendar, signaling a shift to a new one. Not many years before that date, on December 30, 2000, our calendar entered a new millennium, signaling a similar transition. Numerous authors confused this date with the monotheistic concept of the end of the world, regardless. They thought that this Mayan calculation was an estimation of the universal destruction that would end all life on Earth. This, however, was a misinterpretation of the Mayan calculation of prophecy, which sent out a wave of terror among many people, particularly Christians. Those who benefitted, however, were authors, filmmakers, and publishers.

The Norse

The Norse celebrated the Autumnal Equinox with a festival named Haust blót. This term could be translated to Autumn Sacrifice. Many Neo-pagans, especially those who worship and honor the deities of the Norse pantheon, still celebrate this festival. Considering the season's color and essence, with darkness and cold taking over, this prompts communities to large light bonfires. Thus, the Fire element is of great significance. During the celebrations of Haust blót, people would perform fire rituals and base their celebrations around the flames. They covered the fields and pastries in red, orange, and dark yellow fields and believed the red shades found in the sky during dusk to be a symbol of blood. This, they thought, was a warning of the hardship that the harsh winters would bring. It was believed that winter was a challenge presented by the gods themselves, which is why acceptance and resilience were necessary.

Japan

The Japanese traditionally celebrate the Spring and Fall Equinoxes over a period of six days. Six is an important number in Japanese culture, signifying their six ideals: effort, wisdom, perfection, perseverance, giving, and meditation. According to traditional Japanese spiritual beliefs, these qualities are essential before one reaches a higher level of consciousness. To them, the Spring and Fall Equinoxes are both ideal for reflecting and pondering on life's true meaning and essence.

Important Correspondences

Symbols

- Pinecones
- Seeds
- Cornucopia or horn of plenty

Color

- Red
- Orange
- Brown
- Yellow
- Copper
- Dark yellow
- Dark green

Food

- Beans
- Corn
- Apples
- Squash
- Cider
- Pumpkin
- Pomegranate
- Root vegetables
- Wine

Herbs

- Rosehips
- Mugwort
- Rosemary
- Yarrow
- Sage

Plants

- Elderberry
- Chamomile
- Star anise
- Ginger
- White oak bark

Stones

- Aventurine
- Sapphire
- Amber
- Cat's eye
- Jasper

Incense

A Mixture Of:

- Lavender flowers
- Myrrh resin
- Rose petals
- Cinnamon
- Apple peel

Flower

- Thistle
- Marigolds
- Sunflowers

Animals

- Stag
- Owl
- Blackbird
- Salmon

Deities

- Mabon
- Persephone
- Inanna
- Pomona
- Morgan
- Demeter
- Green Man

It is said that the goddess reveals herself in her most abundant, motherly form during the Fall Equinox. The god manifests as the governor of harvest and the king of corn. The deity had sacrificed himself to provide humanity with the last harvest of the year before the winter took over. Mabon aims to honor the deities for their sacrifices and generosity. It is also an opportunity to recognize that the deity will be reborn during Yule. Since most people sustained themselves off farming in the past, this festival was a literal celebration of the harvesting of crops. However, in the modern-day world, people started applying this concept to the manifestation of wishes, aspirations, hopes, and dreams, or the "seeds" they had planted earlier in the year. Rituals that honor the deities should be conducted while reflecting upon everything that has unfolded in your favor. Even if the "harvest" was not abundant, you should still thank the deities for putting in the effort.

Chapter 2: Mabon Deities and Lore

In Celtic mythology, Mabon is the god of youth, music, and the sun. In Welsh literature, he is often referred to as "Maponos," which means Divine Youth, Divine Son, and the Great Son. According to the Gauls, he was the son of Dea Matrona, the embodiment of the triple goddess. In Welsh mythology, Dea Matrona was a personification of Modron, and he is called Mabon ap Modron, which means the Divine son of the Divine Mother. He was also the son of the god of the underworld, Urien. A few legends mention that he had Mabon as a brother. Ancient Celts believed Mabon was associated with light, while his brother was associated with darkness. Mabon also had the title of "The Divine Hunter" because he enjoyed the sport and was known to be one of the best hunters.

It is believed many of the Celtic deities were once real people, and Mabon was no different. One night, three days after his birth, Mabon was kidnapped from his mother, Modron. He was held captive in a Gloucester prison called CaerLoyw, which means "the City of Light." However, no one knows why Mabon was taken from his mother and imprisoned. According to the Culhwch and Olwen story, which narrates his kidnapping, imprisonment, and release, there was a hero called Culhwch. Culhwch fell in love with a woman named Olwen. Olwen's father, Ysbaddaden, set him a series of difficult, and some believed, impossible, quests before he could take his daughter's hand. One such task was to hunt a magical boar. However, he would not be able to find the boar without a specific hunting dog named Drudwyn. No one in the heavens or on Earth could control this dog except for the Divine Hunter himself, Mabon. Finding Mabon was an impossible task in itself because ever since he was kidnapped, no one knew where he was or even if he was dead or alive. Some people did not even know who Mabon was. Or if he was a real person.

Only one person could find Mabon, and that was his cousin, Eiddoel. However, Eiddoel was also imprisoned in Gloucester. Folklore has it that many events took place during the search for Mabon. Culhwch and his friends went around asking all the old and wise animals to help them find him. This fact was emphasized to show that Mabon was ancient, and so was his imprisonment. In fact, it was believed Mabon had been imprisoned since the beginning of time. However, none of the animals knew where he was kept. They came across the oldest salmon (Llyn Lliw) in the water, also the oldest of any animal. He told them that he had heard Mabon wailing in his prison in Gloucester. When Culhwch found this information out, he sought his cousin's help, who just happened to be the legendary King Arthur (other legends referred to Arthur as his uncle).

Arthur, together with his knights, rode together to free Mabon. On arrival in Gloucester, the shouts of pain from Mabon could be heard by all. So, they attacked the prison with hopes of freeing Mabon. They were successful in their endeavors, and Mabon was set free, opting to go and hunt as the first thing to do. He hunted Twrch Trwyth, the great boar, on his great horse, aided by his dog. He killed the boar and used combs and blades fashioned from the boar's tusks and bones to cut Ysbaddaden's hair and shave his beard. Ysbaddaden died shortly after, and the two lovers, Culhwch and Olwen, were finally able to get married.

Mabon became the ruler of Wales and even came to Arthur's aid in the battle of Badon. The god of youth was highly revered by the Celts and Romans alike, and to this day, people speak his name. There is a village and a standing stone in Scotland named after him.

No one knows for a fact if the Mabon Sabbat was named after him, although it makes sense if it is. Mabon is a day to recognize the gods' sacrifices (their deaths and rebirth). The festival takes place in September, right before the dark days of fall and winter, and is a time when people hunt to prepare for these few months. Mabon was the Divine Hunter. With his skills, strengths, and the suffering he endured in prison, his memory should be kept alive. He was also the Sun god, associated with the sun's rebirth after the dark winter days. His imprisonment and eventual release resemble the sun being kept away by the cold and dark winter and finally being set free when spring arrives.

Mabon was talked about in various tales and poems. He was once mentioned as Mabon ap Madron, one of Arthur's knights, and also as Mabon ap Mell, which means Mabon, son of Lighting. This mention links him to Apollo, the sun god, and his father, Zeus, the god of lighting. This explains why the Romans referred to Mabon as Apollo Maponos. He was portrayed in the Mabinogion stories as a kind and giving god who was always there to lend a hand to mankind.

In ancient myth, the boar was used as a symbol for the underworld and the winter. When Mabon defeated the boar in the Culhwch and Olwen story, it represents how the sun defeats the winter every year to bring us light again.

The boar was used as a symbol for the underworld and winter.
https://pixabay.com/es/vectors/jabali-salvaje-animal-38001/

Wine also plays a role on this special day. September is the month or the "Wine Moon." This was a traditional time to harvest the grapes that had been planted earlier in the year. Ancient pagans believed that grapes and wine were sacred as they symbolize transformation and rebirth, which are themes for the Mabon festival. For this reason, many wine deities were linked to it. Now we are going to take a look at all the deities who are associated with the Mabon festival.

Persephone

The Greek goddess Persephone's story is one that captures the spirit of the Mabon festival. The story of her kidnapping at the hands of Hades and how the Earth suffered (as a result) resembles the darkness our world experiences during the winter months. Persephone was the daughter of Demeter, the goddess of harvest and agriculture, and Zeus, the sky god and the chief of all Greek deities.

Statue of Persephone.
*Carole Raddato from Frankfurt, Germany, CC BY-SA 2.0
<https://creativecommons.org/licenses/by-sa/2.0>, via Wikimedia Commons
https://commons.wikimedia.org/wiki/File:Detail_of_Persephone-
Isis,_Statue_group_of_Persephone_(as_Isis)_and_Pluto_(as_Serapis),_from_the_Sanctuar
y_of_the_Egyptian_Gods_at_Gortyna,_mid-
2nd_century_AD,_Heraklion_Archaeological_Museum_(30305161481).jpg*

Persephone was the goddess of fertility. She was known to be a very beautiful girl, and many gods were mesmerized by her beauty and willing to do anything to win her heart. However, Demeter was very protective of her. Some would say she was even obsessed with her daughter, so she did not let any of the gods near her.

Hades, the god of the underworld and brother to Zeus and Demeter, wanted to marry Persephone but Demeter refused. One day, Persephone and her nymphs went to pick flowers. She wandered off alone, and while walking, she saw a strange flower that had a beautiful smell which, according to the legend, was a narcissus flower. As she leaned down to pluck the flower, the ground beneath her feet suddenly opened up, and Persephone fell. She screamed her heart out, but someone caught her in a chariot and rode off. Still screaming for help and scared, Persephone took a look at her captor to find it was Hades, the man she secretly had feelings for.

Needless to say, Demeter was livid and wanted her daughter back. She was heartbroken and miserable and had only one thing in mind, Persephone. She neglected her duties on earth as the goddess of agriculture and harvest, and the earth suffered as a result. People were starving and dying. Zeus saw no other option but to intervene. It is believed that Zeus aided Hades with the kidnapping. He sent for Persephone, who was now married to Hades and became the queen of the underworld and reunited her with her mother. However, Persephone had tasted a pomegranate seed in the underworld. According to the laws of the underworld, anyone who tasted pomegranate could not leave, and so she was stuck in the underworld.

The great god considered a compromise—Persephone would spend a part of her life in the underworld and the rest of the time with her family. All parties agreed to Zeus's decisions. When Persephone was on earth, her mother would rejoice, and the earth would blossom as well. This happened during spring and summer. However, when she went to the underworld, Demeter was consumed with grief, and the earth became barren during the months of fall and winter.

Persephone, like the sun, disappeared during the winter and returned again in the spring. She was both dark and light, and these two parts of her were always fighting with each other, just as Mabon, the light, fought his brother, the darkness.

Demeter

We cannot talk about the autumn equinox without mentioning Demeter, who is responsible for the cycle of the four seasons. The Autumn equinox marks the time when Persephone travels to the underworld and reunites with Hades. It is also the time Demeter spent grieving and abandoned the earth to suffer.

Bust of Demeter.
Museo nazionale romano di palazzo Altemps, CC BY 2.5
<https://creativecommons.org/licenses/by/2.5>, via Wikimedia Commons
https://commons.wikimedia.org/wiki/File:Demeter_Altemps_Inv8596_n2.jpg

The Greeks believed that the gods were responsible for everything. For this reason, they believed Demeter, Persephone, and Hades' story explained the cycle of the four seasons. Demeter was the one responsible for Earth's withering during the months of autumn and winter and its rebirth and transformation during the months of spring and summer.

Hermes

Hermes was the Greek god of the roads, herds, folks, and the souls of the dead. He was also the messenger of the gods. Hermes had a unique gift that made him stand out from any other Olympian god. He was the only one able to cross the border between the living and the dead. Delivering the souls of the dead to Hades allowed Hermes to travel to the underworld. He was even referred to as the "leader of the souls." Hermes played a role in many legends as the messenger of the gods. In fact, he was the one Zeus sent to bring Persephone back from the underworld.

Hermes is associated with Mabon since he was the one who brought Persephone to Demeter, so, in a way, he brought the sun and life back to earth, allowing Demeter to bless the world again. Being able to travel to the underworld meant that Hermes had a light and dark side. You might say Hermes had had a dark side ever since he was an infant. When he was a toddler, he played a trick on his brother Apollo and stole his cattle. He was known as a trickster and enjoyed pranking people. However, he was beloved by the gods, and even his brother Apollo, whom he often tricked.

He wasn't evil per se, but we cannot say that he was good either. He would do anything to amuse himself, no matter the consequences. He could be good just as easily as he could be evil, which is why he was the patron of both thieves and merchants.

Thoth

Thoth was one of the most prominent gods in ancient Egypt. He was the god of writing, the moon, languages, wisdom, medicine, and secrets. Thoth was often compared to Hermes as both gods were associated with communication and wisdom and acted as messengers to the gods. Like his Greek counterpart Hermes, Thoth was also connected to the underworld and able to travel between the realms. In the afterlife, the souls of the dead cannot pass on without a ritual that is referred to as "the weighing of the hearts." Thoth was the one responsible for this ritual by weighing the deceased's heart against a feather of mat. If the scales balanced, this meant they had been a good person who did no harm, so their souls were permitted to move on to the afterlife. However, if the scales were not balanced, then they were sinners whose souls would be devoured by a beast.

Thoth was born from the lips of Ra, the sun god. As the son of the sun god and someone who was able to travel to the underworld and back, Thoth can easily be compared to Mabon, the sun god, and the son of the god of the underworld. Thoth, just like all the gods mentioned, is also celebrated during the Mabon festival.

Dionysus

Dionysus was the Greek god of wine and fertility and patron of the arts. We have mentioned the importance of wine for ancient pagans and how they considered it sacred. Dionysus was the creator of wine which connected him to the Mabon festival as both represent rebirth and transformation. Dionysus' story includes themes of death and rebirth as well. He was the son of Zeus and a mortal woman called Semele. Dionysus was the only god who had a mortal parent. Semele knew that the man she was having an affair with was a god, but she had no idea that it was Zeus, the chief god. When Hera, the goddess of marriage and family and Zeus's wife, found out that her husband was cheating on her, she was consumed with jealousy. Hera disguised herself and went to Semele and persuaded her to talk to the god Zeus and convince him of who he truly was.

Zeus paid a visit to Semele, and she informed him that she had but one desire in her heart, and after some talking, he promised to grant her desire. He was persuaded to show his true form and did so out of love for Semele. Zeus was heartbroken by the request because he knew what would happen if he did, but he also could not go back on his word after taking an oath. When Zeus revealed his true form, Semele as a mortal, was not able to handle his glory, so she was burned to ashes. However, she was pregnant at the time. Zeus saved the fetus and stitched it to his thigh until he was born. The fetus was Dionysus, who became immortal because he was birthed from Zeus, not his mortal mother.

Hera could not cope with the knowledge that the boy her husband had fathered with another woman was still alive and decided to have him killed. She sent the Titans after him, who ripped him apart. However, Rhea, Zeus, and Hera's mother, who was also the mother of the gods, brought Dionysus back to life. Hera could not hurt Dionysus again because Zeus had him protected.

Just as he was brought back to life, Dionysus was one of the few gods who were able to bring the dead back from the underworld. He wanted to meet his mother, who was always on his mind, even though they had never met. So, one day, he traveled to the underworld and brought Semele back. Themes of rebirth are repeated a few times in Dionysus' story, which makes him one of the gods that should be worshiped during the time of the autumn equinox. He was also connected to Demeter as both were considered prominent deities and were very kind towards mankind. Just like the earth, Dionysus was unhappy and would wither during the fall and winter. However, he was full of joy during harvest seasons.

Bacchus

Bacchus was the Roman counterpart of Dionysus as he was also the god of wine. It was believed that Bacchus was the one who was responsible for religious devotion, creativity, and ecstasy. He would also grant drunkenness to anyone who asked for it. Bacchus' birth and rebirth story share many similarities with that of Dionysus. His father, Jupiter, king of the gods in Roman culture, fell in love with the goddess of agriculture, Prosperina, Persephone in Greek culture. Jupiter took the form of a snake, sneaked into the underworld, and made love with Prosperina. As a result, Bacchus was conceived. However, he was first called Liber. Liber/Bacchus was one of the Roman gods who fought during the battle of Titanomachy. During one of these battles, Liber was killed, and like his Greek counterpart, he was torn apart.

Jupiter, who was consumed with grief, took his son's remains and placed his heart in a potion. He then gave the potion with the pieces of the heart inside to the king of Thebes' wife, who was called Semele and who was also a mortal. Semele drank the potion and became pregnant. However, just like in Dionysus' story, Semele was murdered because of Juno, Jupiter's wife and chief goddess. Jupiter took the fetus from Semele's womb and sewed him to his thigh until he was born. He was born Bacchus. Just like Dionysus, the story is about birth, death, and transformation, which are the themes of the autumn equinox.

Cernunnos

Cernunnos was one of the most prominent Celtic deities. He was the god of wild places, nature, fertility, and beasts. Cernunnos was also referred to as "the Horned One." Not much is known about him because many of his myths have been lost. For this reason, he is often considered more of a mysterious god. He often acted as a mediator between nature and man. The Horned One was also considered the lord of life and death and experienced death and rebirth. Cernunnos, just like mankind, would grow old over time. However, instead of dying and perishing, he would start over and begin a new cycle of life, just like earth and the four seasons, with the earth transforming or dying during the winter to come back to life in the spring.

The Morrigan

The Morrigan was the goddess of war, death, and witchcraft. It is believed that she was a triple goddess and went by many names like

Morrigu, The Morrigan goddess, and Thye Great Queen. She could predict which soldiers would die in a battle. She would usually appear on battlefields taking the form of a crow to motivate the soldiers and frighten their enemies.

As mentioned, The Morrigan was a triple goddess and existed between life and death. One aspect of the triple goddess was Macha, who was a horse goddess. She came back from the dead to predict the future. The second aspect of the triple goddess is Badb, who was the Crone goddess of the underworld. The third aspect of her is Anu, who was the mother of gods. The Morrigan can also be associated with the Mabon festival with themes of death and rebirth. As one of her aspects came back from the dead, which represented rebirth, and the other was the goddess of the underworld, The Morrigan represented themes of rebirth and death, which are what the autumn equinox is all about.

Mabon's story is both sad and exciting. Being imprisoned all his life, Mabon was saved from danger and spent his days helping mankind. Full of mystery and bravery, Moban was an interesting and popular figure featured in various Welsh, Celt, and Gallic literature legends. Although some people believe that the Celts never celebrated Mabon, and this is more of a modern idea, Mabon represented many things associated with the autumn equinox, like transformation and rebirth. It is believed that Mabon was simply a hero in an Arthurian legend, while there are others who believe Mabon and Maponos are not the same people and that Maponos is a god while Mabon is mortal. However, we can all agree the story of Mabon is fascinating, and its festival is a special day to give thanks to mother earth,

All the deities mentioned here symbolize the earth's transformation and rebirth that occur annually. When celebrating this special day, make sure you call upon any of the gods connected to Mabon.

Chapter 3: Magical Fruits, Herbs, and Flowers

Now that you are familiar with the myths and lore surrounding Mabon, you can understand how some special fruits, flowers, and plants came to play a significant role in the festival. Not only are they used to decorate an altar, but they are also important ingredients in various Mabon rituals and rites. The great Mabon feast also comprises various recipes using these specific fruits to pay tribute to the season's harvest. These fruits, flowers, and herbs have unique symbolism and meanings, making the festival even more special. This chapter will dive into the many types of fruits, herbs, and flowers used in the Mabon festivities.

Magical Fruits

Mabon is a harvest festival, and numerous fruits and other crops that flourish in this season are integral to the festival.

Some fruits are considered to be magical.
https://unsplash.com/photos/K0efSg5xy9w

These magical fruits are deeply connected with the ancient lore associated with Mabon. Over time, the use of these fruits has become common in the tradition, followed faithfully by all who celebrate it. Some of the most famous Mabon fruits include:

1. Apples

Apples are the main fruit symbol for this season. They have been used for centuries in many sacred traditions, symbolizing life, healing, renewal, regeneration, and health. Where did you think the saying, "An apple a day keeps the doctor away." came from? This fruit also has a deep symbolic meaning connected to the lore surrounding Persephone and Demeter. Demeter being the goddess of earth, and a nurturing soul, used to present people with apples, the fruit of life.

From a pagan perspective, apples are widely loved symbols representing health and vitality. When cut widthways, the center seeds show a pentagon, which according to pagan tradition, represents air, water, earth, fire, and spirit at the top. Apples are used in various dishes and food items for Mabon, including apple pies, roasted apples, apple stuffing, and apple cider.

2. Pears

Pears go along perfectly with Mabon festivities and are one of the most prolific fruits found in the autumn harvest. Many pagans consider pears to be the true harbinger of fall. Cultivated pears go far back in history, with countless recipes evident in every culture. Pears have also been considered sacred in many cultures, but most prominently so in ancient pagan civilizations. The slightly curvy shape of pears echoes the feminine shape and is how they became associated with the feminine body, Aphrodite, goddess of love. Mabon feasts have a fine selection of pear dishes, ranging from simple pear slices to delicious baked pears or pear tarts.

3. Persimmons

Persimmons are less familiar woodland fruits and have been used for Mabon feasts and festivities for centuries. These sweet and slightly chewy fruits add a delicious flavor to Mabon recipes. Moreover, they are used to create scents, especially to be used during Mabon festivities. This fruit has numerous health benefits and is largely associated with Demeter's harvest in a pagan culture. Recipes range from sweet persimmon jams and muffins to savory persimmon risotto.

4. Pomegranate

Pomegranates deserve special mention with regards to the autumn equinox festival. You have read the story of Persephone and Demeter's tragic love in the previous chapter, and while there are many variations in this story, pomegranate fruits have a prominent role in them. Hades used pomegranate seeds to trick Persephone into staying in the underworld. This is why pomegranates are often called the fruit of death. It was served to

Persephone and made her stay in the underworld. Modern Mabon festivities have many pomegranate dishes as part of the feasts. These fruits are not just good for health reasons; they are also quite tasty and symbolize the lore associated with Mabon. Pomegranate juice is also a famous beverage for Mabon festivities.

5. Grapes

The autumnal equinox has a special place for grapes because there would be no wine without them. Pagan myths and lore are full of stories and tales that involve wine and the gods. It is used to honor themselves and many other beings. These mainly include Dionysus, Bacchus, and other fermentation deities. According to Wiccan culture, grapevines are associated with fertility and magic and can also be used in fertility rituals. Mabon marks the perfect time for the ripening of wines, and so wines have long been used as a sacred symbol during this festival. This time is also when new wines are set up to ferment. So, if you are hosting a Mabon event, be sure to get a large barrel of wine for everyone to drink. Grapes can also be served fresh or added to fruit salads and other recipes.

6. Berries

Mabon berries include wild damsons, rosehips, sloes, elderberries, hawthorn berries, blackberries, and more. They are not only used to symbolize the rich harvest provided by the goddess Demeter but also symbolize the sweetness in life. Various berries are included in the feast in the form of jams, juices, smoothies, margaritas, baked items, and frozen items. They can also be used to decorate the Mabon altar in a cornucopia. The cornucopia itself is a significant symbol for Mabon. Also called the horn of plenty, the cornucopia is filled with Mabon fruits to represent the wealth of the harvest season.

Magical Flowers

The autumn equinox or Mabon is largely associated with the mythical lore of Demeter, Persephone, and Hades. When Persephone was kidnapped and taken to the Underworld, Demeter's sorrow and rage destroyed nature on earth. As soon as Persephone was allowed to return to earth, Demeter was overjoyed and restored all the plants, herbs, and flowers to full bloom. This is how flowers became deeply connected to festivities during the autumnal equinox. Many very pretty flowers are associated with Mabon festivities, and they are used for both decorations and rituals. These are some of the flowers most often chosen for Mabon festivities.

1. Asters

Asters are one of the most prolific seen during Mabon festivities. Asters can be found in many colors, from pale reds to bright purples. The most common aster color associated with the autumnal equinox is blue

These symbolize devotion, loyalty, and abundance. In addition to being used in decorations, these flowers are often used to encourage metaphysical spiritualism in celebratory rituals. This flower is usually associated with the goddess Aphrodite and is thus used in love spells and rituals. These rituals can be done during Mabon to increase the intensity of the manifested power. They can also be used in tarot card readings and other similar rituals.

2. Chrysanthemum

Chrysanthemums are often used for protective purposes, especially *metaphysical protection*, and come in handy when you are dealing with the spirit world. They are a significant part of Mabon, and their petals are used to decorate the equinox altar. They are also used in rituals and herbal recipes. The unique thing about this flower is that it is available in a range of colors, and each is used to symbolize different things. For instance, white chrysanthemums represent healing and purification, whereas red or purple ones are associated with passion and power. Yellow and orange shades depict the sun's fiery energy.

To use these flowers in your Mabon festival, you can make wreaths or hoops to hang on your home's front door or windows for protection. You can also use this flower's yellow, orange, and red shades to create an autumn equinox crown for yourself.

3. Sunflowers

Sunflower seeds are sown naturally in fertile soil in springtime and reach full bloom during early September. As these flowers grow, they turn their face toward the sun, demonstrating the divine power of the sun. And as the center of the flowers begins to swell, its petals begin to droop and wither until the flower turns back towards the ground, from where it started. The birth, growth, death, and rebirth of these flowers represent nature's cycle, which is associated with the goddess of the harvest, Demeter.

4. Thistles

Another flower most commonly associated with Mabon is the thistle, mainly used for protective spells and rituals. It can also be used to improve your financial and spiritual blessings. You can do many rituals and spells during the autumnal equinox using the thistle flower or seeds to improve your chances. Throw these flowers in a fire to have a protective shield around you that protects you from natural elements like lightning. The beautiful flower represents vitality, joy, energy, and protection. If not used for rituals, you can always use thistle flowers to decorate your Mabon altar.

5. Marigold

This gorgeous flower is not only suited for Mabon decorations, but it is also useful in many natural remedies and, naturally, pagan rituals. Marigold flowers are associated with the element of fire, and the sun, both symbols of autumn and Mabon season. Marigolds have magical properties attributed that make them perfect to be used for rituals and spells during Mabon. These include clairvoyance, psychic readings, prophecies, love, dreams, and renewing of personal energy. The best time to do these rituals would be at noon on the autumnal equinox. The flower can also be used as an herb and has many medicinal applications as well. These include treating swelling and inflammation or healing sprains or wounds.

6. Russian Sage

Sage is one of the most common flowers used in pagan and Wiccan rituals and rites. This is mainly because of the plant's healing and purifying properties which make it irreplaceable for many modern pagans. Almost every pagan festival makes use of sage flowers in one way or another. You can simply use sage to physically and spiritually clean your home. This ritual, known as smudging, can be done by burning sage and wafting its smoke throughout your house. Mainly used for protective, prosperity, and clarity spells, sage is considered to bring health and vitality. However, when using it for magical purposes, you should not cut sage with a metal knife. Rather, it should be plucked.

7. Hydrangea

For Mabon celebrations, you can use hydrangea flowers and leaves to create beautiful scenic decorations within and outside your house. These could include wreaths, flower bouquets, leaf paintings, or simply bunch them together for a colorful arrangement. Hydrangea flowers are often used for banishing purposes and are more common at Samhain but are also used throughout the autumnal equinox to banish any evil entities coming your way. They are associated with psychic shielding, moon magic, and purification.

Magical Plants and Herbs

Magical plants and herbs also play a major part in Mabon festivities, preparations, and the sacred day itself. Demeter's association with nature is the main connection between plants, herbs, and Mabon. These are used throughout the festival to perform different rites and rituals. Plants are said to have not just healing and therapeutic properties for physical ailments but also work wonders for your spiritual healing. Some of the most common plants and herbs associated with the autumnal equinox include:

1. Lavender

Lavender has been used for centuries in pagan rituals, especially during the time of the autumnal equinox. Rumor has it that this herb is used to encourage healthy communication and attracts love and serenity. This herb also has well-known medicinal uses, as it helps reduce inflammation and also soothes burns and bites. For Mabon, you can make a lavender essential oil blend to sprinkle around the house or make some delicious herbal tea to soothe your – or your guests' - nerves. To use as decoration, bundle up sprigs of lavender with other herbs and place them near the Mabon altar. You can create an incense blend to reflect and purify your energy for ceremonial purposes.

2. Grapevine

As you know by now, grapes are a symbol of abundance and fertility. A healthy and abundant grape harvest signifies a prosperous year ahead. In modern practices, many Wiccans and pagans use grapevines for various ritualistic purposes. Some ways you can incorporate grape vines into your Mabon rituals and decorations include:

- Wrap the beautiful grape vines around the altar, or create garlands out of these plants

- Make a simple grapevine pentacle to hang on your wall

- Use grape leaves in your rituals and spells to bring abundance and fertility to your crops

- To create a simple good luck charm, wrap a grape leaf around a silver coin and tie this with a green string.; keep this talisman in your pocket to bring you prosperity.

3. Witch Hazel

Witch hazel is one of the most commonly used herbs in witchcraft and ritualistic practices. It has countless herbal and medicinal uses, including treating poisons, rashes, sunburns, inflammation, eczema, acne, burns, bruises, eye strains, achy muscles, bruises, insects' bites, and sprains. Witch hazel is often referred to as the wound healer herb. It can be blended with other herbs or incense for ritualistic purposes to keep away evil spirits and anyone harboring ill intentions.

4. Rose

Rose is the ultimate herb to use in love spells and rituals. Also, one of the autumnal equinox herbs, rose herbs, have various therapeutic properties, most often used for treating skin diseases and enhancing beauty. For ritualistic purposes, rose herbs can be used to lift your mood and help open up your creative space. So, if you are an artist with a block, perform a ritualistic cleansing with rose herbs to open up your creative channel.

5. Cinnamon

This spice can mean spiritual happiness, wealth, and peace. It was an ingredient used a lot in harvest celebrations as apples were bountiful, and cinnamon pairs well with them. The spice is still plentiful today and used as a flavoring in pies, offers, and other autumnal foods and drinks. The spice also provides many health benefits, from aiding digestion to managing cholesterol. So, even if you overindulge with the Mabon feast, cinnamon added to various dishes will be a useful balm against this habit. Cinnamon can be added to incense for ceremonial purposes to purify the house and even outdoors.

6. Oak

One of the better-known symbols of the equinox, Oaks are known for their many herbal and ritualistic uses during the Mabon season. Oak used to be one of three sacred druidic deities and has many magical properties for use in various spells and rituals. Medicinal uses include treating hemorrhoids, or sinus infections, whereas ritualistic purposes include positive manifestations of healing, longevity, power, order, protection, love, financial success, fertility, and fortune. You can perform a protective ritual involving oak acorns and place them near your windows to ward off lightning or other natural disasters.

7. Myrrh

As it is associated with multiple goddesses, myrrh is one of the most sacred herbs of Mabon and is used to heighten your spirituality. Myrrh is sacred to the Egyptian goddess Isis, as well as Demeter. It can thus be used for various ritualistic purposes during the Mabon season, including protection spells, healing rituals, blessings and meditation rites, and consecration of objects like rings, amulets, crystals, and other ritualistic tools. To purify and protect an area, you can burn myrrh plants and use their smoke for the purpose.

8. Passionflower

As its name indicates, Passionflower has herbal and magical uses in protection and love magic. When this herb is used, it brings peace and calmness to your home. For protection rituals, you can dry these flowers and sprinkle them over the doorstep or right in front of your home's front door to keep harm away. Burning these herbs can help promote love and understanding between people. You can also use this herb to create love potions.

9. Calendula

Calendula flowering herbs were named after the ancient Romans and have been used for healing and magical purposes for more than a century. These herbs are used to release feelings of joy and happiness and bring strength to a weak heart. You can use these plants for a ritual bath during the autumnal equinox to attract praise and admiration from others. You can also make spell bags consisting of calendula flowers to attract success and be triumphant in love-related matters. Its herbal uses include the treatment of skin rashes, insect bites, sunburns, and minor infections.

10. Peppermint

Peppermint has many therapeutic and magical properties, which has kept this herb on the front line for ritualistic and healing purposes for many years. Associated with purification, healing, protection, and love, peppermint herbs can be used in many ritualistic practices ranging from aura cleaning to home purification during the sacred time of Mabon.

Chapter 4: Crafts and Decorations

Any festive occasion is incomplete without matching festive decor to get you in the mood for the festival. And this is true for the autumnal equinox celebrations. Mabon is a time of joy and happiness, and to celebrate it fully, there should be ample amounts of decorations and crafts. The best way to pay tribute to this joyous occasion is to create crafts and decorations that have a significant meaning for a holiday. So, whether you are celebrating the autumnal equinox as a Wiccan practitioner or a pagan, there are many DIY crafts that you can make to add a celebratory air to your Mabon festival. In this chapter, we discuss themed Mabon crafts and give you easy step-by-step guides on how to make your own special decorations. You will also learn the background, how items became associated with the autumnal equinox and its traditions.

Autumn Fairy

This autumn fairy dolly is created with natural materials, which are all connected with Mabon's theme. Whether you believe in fairies or not, they are a symbol of the mythological lore associated with Mabon. This cute piece will not just make an interesting curiosity for the little ones but will also add a whimsical charm to your Mabon altar.

Materials Needed:

- Autumn leaves (red, orange, brown, green, and yellow shades)
- Pine cone (small or medium-sized)
- Acorn cap (large sized)
- Rusty-colored orange wool
- White felt (1 ball)
- String (small piece)
- Hot glue gun

Steps:

1. First, prepare the fairy's head with the white felt ball. You can also use a large cotton wool ball in its place.
2. Use the rusty orange wool to make the fairy's hair by parting the wool into two parts. Glue the hair on top of the white felt ball. Hold it until the glue has dried.
3. Now, take the acorn cap and stick it on top of the fairy's hair with the glue gun. Hold it in place until stuck.
4. Use the pinecone to make the fairy's body. Place it upside down and add glue to the base of the pinecone. Stick the fairy's head here and let it dry.
5. Take two bright-colored autumn leaves to make the fairy's wings. Make sure that the leaves you pick are equal in size. Stick these to the back of the pinecone from the stem side.
6. Tie a string to the acorn's stem to hang the dolly wherever you want.

Apple Garland

As discussed in the previous chapters, apples have long been associated with the magical time of Mabon. They are not just used in food but also to make various decor items as well. Garlands are one of the most common decorations during Mabon festivities. They add a touch of nature to your house and are not that hard to make or purchase.

Materials Needed:

- Oranges (3 to 5)

- Apples (2 to 3)

- Bay leaves (15 to 20)

- Cinnamon sticks (1 bag)

- Twines (arm's length)

- Embroidery needles

- Foil

- Cookie sheet

- Oven

Steps:

1. First, cut the oranges and apples into thin slices. Use a sharp knife to do this; otherwise, the slices will be uneven. The apples will resemble hearts when cut perfectly, and the orange slices will be circular.

2. Place these slices between drying sheets and press to squeeze the juice out. This makes the drying process much easier.

3. Preheat the oven to high heat, and slide in the fruit slices arranged neatly on cookie sheets. Turn over the slices every few minutes to avoid burning.

4. Once the fruit slices are done being dried, line up the materials together and start to put a piece of twine through them.

5. Add the orange slices, apple slices, and cinnamon sticks to the garland, one at a time. Once done, hang it on your doors or simply on the wall.

Candy Corn Pine Cones

Pine cones are pretty common around Mabon season, and a combination of pine cones and candy corn is the perfect craft for this festive day. Pine cones are great for decorating purposes, especially during the fall season. Combine this with beautifully applied paint and glitter, and you have got the perfect eye-catching decoration for your autumnal equinox festival.

Materials Needed:

- Pine cones
- Parchment paper
- Oven
- Spray paint
- Glitter
- Mod Podge

Steps:

1. First, arrange the pine cones on a parchment sheet and heat them in the oven at low heat for about 30 minutes. This will help kill any critters or insects that may have survived the harvest.

2. Start by painting the first layer using orange spray paint. Make sure you cover the whole pine cone with the paint.

3. After the first coat has dried, take the white spray paint, and spray the tip of the pine cone white.

4. Once the white coat has dried, hold the top of the pine cone, and spray the bottom with yellow spray paint.

5. Let the pine cones dry overnight, and then use a mod podge and brush to apply the glitter to the cones.

6. Put the pine cones in baskets or decorate the Mabon altar with them however you would like.

Waxed Fall Leaves

Is there anything more beautiful than the different shaded autumn leaves that fall to the ground during the autumnal equinox? If you are an admirer of the vibrant colored leaves of fall, this craft is perfect for creating an inexpensive yet stunning look.

Materials Needed:

- Fall leaves

- Mini crock pocket

- Paraffin wax

Steps:

1. Melt the paraffin wax in the mini crock pot or any other container and pour the melted wax onto a sheet.

2. Start dipping the leaves in the wax. Be careful not to let your fingers touch the hot wax while doing so.

3. Let the leaves stay there until the wax dries completely. This should take a minute or so.

4. You can make more than one coat on the leaves for a more solid foundation. About 2 to 3 coats should be enough for this purpose.

5. Once they are done, you can place them wherever you would like. For instance, place them on the Mabon altar or the dinner table, or string them on a thread to make a garland. You can also paint these waxed leaves to make them more vibrant and aesthetic.

Apple Candles

Again, as apples are closely associated with Mabon and Harvest goddess Demeter, and seeing that they are plentiful at this time of the year, Mabon wouldn't be Mabon without them. To make the most of these fruits, you should use as many as you can, not just in the grand Mabon feast but also in your crafts and decorations. One such craft can be these creative apple candles. The best part is, they are super easy to make! This craft doesn't even need a lot of supplies, time, or effort on your part but ends up being one of the most creative crafts on Mabon.

Materials Needed:

- Apples
- Tea lights/Candles
- Hole saw
- Spoon

Steps:

1. Take an apple and wash, and dry it completely. Red apples will be perfect to match the theme, but green or yellow ones will work just as well.

2. Use a hole saw bit to drill out a circular hole the size of the candle top from the apple. Make sure you make an accurately sized hole to match your candle or tea light, or the craft will end up looking uneven.

3. Use a spoon to pry out the extra material from the hole you made.

4. Finally, place the candle inside the hole until it sits snugly inside. Light the candles and place them wherever you would like.

Acorn Wreath

If you want a simplistic yet beautiful-looking wreath for your front door, an acorn wreath would be the perfect thing. It is not just easy and inexpensive to make; it also matches the theme of the autumn equinox celebration. Acorns are another of the symbolic food items that are associated with Mabon.

Acorn wreath.

https://pixabay.com/cs/photos/guirnalda-oto%c3%b1o-corona-oto%c3%b1o-3041838/

Materials Needed:

- Acorns (large or similar-sized)

- Hot glue gun

- Floral wreath

Steps:

1. Gather as many acorns as you can find. If you can't find some close to your home, order some online.

2. Wash and dry the acorns to clean them, and then put them in the oven at low heat for 30 minutes to get rid of any insects infesting them.

3. Use the glue guns to glue the acorns to the straw or wooden wreaths one by one. Make sure there are no gaps, and every space has an acorn in it.

4. Use a ribbon to hang the wreath on your front door. If you want, spray-paint the acorns any color you like. White works best against a darker background.

Leaf Sun-Catcher

Leaves are a major symbol of the fall season and are seen all around the Mabon festivities. There are all kinds of crafts involving leaves that are not just creative but also easy to make, and this one is no exception. This decor will showcase autumn's real beauty using leaves of various colors, shapes, and sizes.

Materials Needed:

- Fall leaves
- Laminator
- Laminating sheets
- Yarn
- Hole punch
- Rubber band
- Scissors
- Masking tape
- Stick

Steps:

1. Go outside and collect some leaves and a three-foot-long stem from a bush. Make sure you cut off all the little twigs from the stick before you bring it home.

2. As for the leaves, make sure they are straight and moist, do not collect dry or curled-up leaves.

3. Let the stick soak in some warm water to make it easier to bend when you make the sun catcher.

4. While the stick is soaking, pick out the most beautiful leaves that you have collected and place them individually in the middle of the laminating paper. Laminate away!

5. Bend the soaked stick slowly into a circle. Make sure that you do it gently so that the stick does not break. Tie the two ends together.

6. Cut the laminated sheet in a circular shape while keeping the leaf in the middle.

7. Punch holes in the edges of the sheet and use masking tape to temporarily hold the laminated leaf between the circular stick.

8. Thread the yarn through the punched holes, and tie it around the stick to hold the laminated piece between the circles.

9. Hang this sun catcher somewhere in direct sunlight so that the colors of the leaf are enhanced.

Cornucopia Basket

As discussed in the previous chapter, cornucopia baskets are hugely symbolic of the autumnal equinox. They are used to store various Mabon fruits, nuts, and charms. Cornucopia baskets symbolize the abundance of harvest and bounty and are thus important features in a Mabon festival. So, this easy-to-make cornucopia basket will be the perfect addition to your Mabon decorations.

Materials Needed:

- Wicker cornucopia (2 ft. long)

- Burlap (2 yards)

- Raffia (200g packages)

- Binder clip

- Spool of jute string

- Hot glue gun

- Scissors

Steps:

1. Wrap the burlap sack around the wicker cornucopia to cover the entire basket, and tuck the extra material inside. Cut away and burlap that hangs over the edges to neaten it.

2. Use adhesive to stick the burlap to the frame. Make sure you secure the whole thing perfectly.

3. Now, it is time to make the ropes to cover the cornucopia. Take your raffia and bind it with the string to create a long length of raffia cord. Take your jute and bind both ends to each other. You will need to create 9-10 of these for the frame—until it is covered.

4. Now wrap these raffia ropes around the cornucopia basket and hot glue the edges to secure them to the frame. Make sure that you add enough glue to the ropes to tightly secure them to the basket.

Mabon Corn Dolly

Considered to be one of the most sacred symbols of Mabon, corn dollies have been historically significant throughout Wiccan and pagan traditions. Early practitioners believed that the spirit of the grain, or harvest, lived in the field with the crops. However, once all the crops were reaped, she no longer had a place to stay. So, the last sheaves were reaped and used to make corn dollies to preserve the spirit of the harvest and keep her safe and warm all winter. When spring came, the corn dolly would be put back into the earth to bring fertility to the land. Many of these traditions have remained almost the same throughout these years. Thus, the corn dolly still has spiritual significance and is a common part of Mabon rituals. Plus, they are pretty easy to make and do not require more than three materials.

Materials Needed:

- Corn husk
- Scissors
- Embroidery thread

Steps:

1. First, you need to soak the husks for a few hours to make them more pliable. Once they have soaked enough, take them out and pat them dry with a towel.

2. Now, select 3 or 4 of the husks that are similar in size. Tie a string around the narrow part of the husks. Secure the knot twice, and then start folding the layers downward.

3. Tie a string around the upper part of the husk where her neck should be. Use another husk for the arms. Roll the husk tightly and push the arms all the way under her neck.

4. Use another piece of thread to tie her middle to resemble a torso. Now, take two long, thin pieces of husk, tie them around her shoulders, and bring them to the front. This will

be her shawl. Use another piece of string to secure her shawl to the front.

5. Quickly put the corn dolly configuration in the oven to dry the husks properly so that they do not shrivel.

6. Take a stick and some twigs to make a miniature broom for the corn dolly.

Mabon Broom

Mabon is a sacred time and is filled with ritualistic cleansing and purification. This is where brooms or besoms come in. You are probably aware that brooms have been associated with witchcraft for centuries, but do you know why that is? It is because brooms or besoms are often used for hand fasting or cleansing ceremonies, especially during sacred times like Mabon. Thus, crafting a styled besom broom will be the perfect addition to your Mabon festival.

Materials Needed:

- A stick
- Pine needles, grass, or straw
- Natural twine
- Hot glue gun

Steps:

1. Gather the pine needles around the base of your stick. Make sure some of the portions of the stick are completely submerged in the pine needles.

2. Now, place this configuration on twine, and tie it around the pine needles and the stick. Make double knots to secure the broom.

3. To further secure the broom, pour some hot glue on the back of the twine knot. Now, carefully wind the twine around the broom in a circular manner. This should completely secure the twine around the broom.

4. To make your besom special, you can decorate it using gemstones, dried flowers, ribbons, or even old jewelry.

5. Anoint your broom with essential oil and ritualistic blessings of Mabon.

Twine-Wrapped Pears

Pears are another symbolic fruit associated with Mabon. They are used extensively in Mabon festivities and are used to celebrate a successful harvest. While this object does not make use of real pears, it is used to represent the pear shapes and perfectly match the theme of the autumnal equinox. Plus, it is a recycling project and makes the perfect way to reuse old light bulbs. Stick them in the cornucopia basket or somewhere on the Mabon altar to add a rustic touch to your decor.

Materials Needed:

- Old light bulbs
- Twine
- Small stick
- Scissors
- Hot glue gun

Steps:

1. First, to make the stem of the pear, use the hot glue gun to fix the small stick to the narrower side of the light bulb.

2. Now, put some hot glue right next to the end of the stem, and glue one end of your twine there.

3. Start wrapping the twine around the body of the light bulb, adding hot glue once in a while to make the wrapping solid. Make sure that you do not leave any space between the twine so that no part of the light bulb is visible.

4. Keep doing this until you reach the bottom of the pear and finally secure the other end of the twine with glue.

5. Voila! You are done. If you want, you can add shades of green and yellow to these twine pears for a more realistic look.

Crafts and decorations are an essential part of any celebratory event. Add to that the sacred symbolism in Wiccan and Pagan celebrations, and these crafts become irreplaceable. While many of the above crafts are mainly used for decorative purposes, some bring ritualistic significance to the table as well. Plus, all of these crafts are pretty easy to make and require little to no supplies.

Chapter 5: Setting Up Your Mabon Altar

Not all pagans consider setting up an altar as a fundamental part of their practice, but those who do, agree that having a sacred space has many advantages. In this chapter, you will learn about the benefits of setting up an altar in your home and how to use this sacred space in your Mabon celebrations. We will suggest several beginner-friendly tips on how to care for your altar before, during, and after the festivities. It is important to note that the advice from this chapter should only serve as *general guidelines.* As with any other magic-enhancer tool, an altar only enhances your powers. It is definitely recommended that you add your personal touch to the space to fully empower your altar, helping you achieve all your magical goals at the second harvest.

The Purposes of an Altar

For most people, an altar is viewed as a collection of objects placed strategically in a purposeful place. For pagans, however, this space signifies much more than that. It provides a connection to nature, spiritual guides, or any other entity you want to communicate with during your practice. The objects you place on your altar and the place itself are also emotionally, mentally, and spiritually linked to you. Moreover, the surface where you lay your magical tools becomes your sacred space, regardless of its size and purpose. Altars come in many shapes and sizes, depending on their intent, type of practice, and place you have available.

The Benefits of a Sacred Space

As in other religions and practices, a spiritual center for one's practice is a critical part of pagan traditions. Having a sacred place dedicated to your practice comes with many benefits for you, your magic, and those around you. Here are some of the gifts you can gain by setting up an altar in your home.

Inviting Positive Energy

We have already established that an altar is a space where you can harness spiritual energy whenever it is needed in your practice. However, it must be noted that it can also serve as a tool for permanently inviting and retaining this positive energy in your home. Setting up an altar at times like Mabon will ensure that the positive energy keeps flowing through your space, following you wherever you happen to be in your home.

Invoking Spirituality

Paganism is a spirituality-based practice, and each object you place on your altar has a connection to your spirit and the spirit of the entities you want to evoke. They represent emotions, intentions, and symbols of deities and spiritual guides that can help you deepen your own spirituality. Even if you are not familiar with spiritual practices, building an altar will help you get in touch with your inner self. The more times you repeat this, the more spiritual power you garner for your magical practice. From the first stone you put on the altar to the first candle you see flickering in front of you, it will all touch your spirit. It will also help you connect with the spirit of whatever entity with which you are working. Earth-based altar decorations like those used at Mabon often include simple items that enhance spirituality. Growing your spirituality involves using your altar for several days, often placing new items on the sacred surface each day. Whether you opt for exchanging the existing ones or adding new objects depends on the purpose of the ritual. Either way, it will enhance the power of the practice and deepen your spiritual connection to it. If your act involves many people, their contribution to a common altar deepens the spiritual bonds within their community, whether they share the same beliefs.

Expressing Your Creativity

Setting a sacred place for your practice is a form of art. Figuring out which items will give you the best results needs a lot of creative thought, even if you have a guideline like the one provided in this chapter. However, we will teach you how to take a creative approach to every situation in your practice and even in day-to-day life. At the same time, it allows you to create something of your own and express your thoughts and emotions through your creation. Whether you draw, write or craft, you can do something for yourself and the cause your altar is dedicated to at any given moment. As your art is also something to be harvested, placing your creations on the altar during Mabon, along with the offerings and symbols, will enhance the spiritual connection to this Sabbat.

Turning Negatives into Positives

Part of the lure of pagan practices is that they allow you to turn negative experiences into positive ones. By building an altar, you gain a space where you can do something about negative influences, regardless of their source. Whether the negativity comes from living beings or malicious spirits, having a sacred place will empower you to fight them and keep them away from you and your space.

Learning Symbols

There is no better way to learn the correct use of existing pagan symbols than displaying them in a space you visit regularly. And this applies not only to written characters but also to colors, animals, and the favorite items of your spiritual guides. Learning the symbols will teach you their purpose and let you see how they work best. This information will help you create your own symbolism in the future with symbols you will have come to know intimately.

Creating a Meditation Center

Whether you wish to devote your practice to a particular spiritual guide, nature itself, or to developing your spirituality in another direction, an altar can be the perfect place for mindfulness practices. By bringing together the right combination of elements, you can create a space where you can unwind after a busy day at work. As the spirits you choose to evoke your senses, your body and mind relax, and your experience becomes deeper. You can use specific symbols geared toward helping you focus your intent on relaxation or, better yet, choose the ones that feel right for you to use in this situation. There is no better way to ground yourself than by meditating in front of the offerings dedicated to the spirits that allowed you to have a bountiful harvest.

Focusing on Your Magical Intentions

Whether you practice magic daily or only during the major pagan celebrations, having a sacred space can help you focus on your intent every time. The way to choose to set an altar sets the tone for each spell you choose to cast, divination technique, or ritual you perform. If you practice magic with others, an altar can bring each person's intention together and focus it on the intended purpose. And if you are a solitary practitioner, you can tailor the space to your specific taste and preferences, which also helps enhance your magical powers.

Remembering Your Ancestors

Pagans regularly turn to spiritual guidance for answers, particularly when they find themselves in a difficult situation in life. That said, the collective wisdom of ancestors can be a great empowerment tool for your practice on any day of your life. Before Mabon, you can ask your ancestral spirits about their practices and better understand this Sabbat with their help. Or you can simply devote your altar to remembering loved ones who have passed away. Create a space that is a reminder of their presence in your life, and they will accompany you on your life's journey. At Mabon, this can include your ancestors' favorite colors or food, an object which they cherished during their life, or whatever item you associate with a particular person. Pagans who practice in groups often choose to add details symbolizing several ancestors and express their gratitude to each of them individually.

Welcoming Nature into Your Life

Establishing a connection with nature is another way to develop your spirituality and empower your practice. Many pagans choose to grow medicinal herbs and plants for food, even if they only do this in a small corner of their home. By placing your harvest bounty in a special place, you can express gratitude for them, which will bring you closer to nature. An altar can be the perfect spot to display these items. Here, you can also use them to channel nature's power to gain insight, cast a spell, or perform any other magical act. Whichever way you choose to connect with nature, you will most likely leave the offerings on the altar for a number of hours and days. This allows the spirits of nature to notice them and provide many blessings in return.

Sharing the Magic

Whether introducing someone to pagan practices or finding common ground with another experienced practitioner, decorating an altar together can be a great way to share your spiritual beliefs. This is common practice for celebrating major Sabbats in larger pagan communities. Helping you set up an altar for a specific purpose is also the perfect way to share the magic of nature with children.

Where to Set Up Your Sacred Space

Before you start setting up your altar, you must choose a suitable place for it. Ideally, it should be away from any high-traffic areas or possible distractions. Otherwise, you will not be able to relax, let alone focus on your intention during your practice. Many pagans choose to set up their altars in their home office or bedroom, as these are the rooms where they spend most of their time. Having a sacred place in your bedroom would also facilitate morning and evening prayers and quick divinations if your practice includes them. If you do not have much space for a full table to serve as an altar, you can always set up a smaller area on your dresser, vanity table, or even inside your closet. If your practices involve mediation, yoga, or similar activities, it is a good idea to set up an altar in a room that can also accommodate these. A functional basement, garden, backyard, patio, and deck areas are also suitable for setting up an altar. In fact, many pagans prefer having a sacred space outside of their home as this makes them feel closer to nature and appreciate its grounding and empowering effects even more.

How to Set Up Your Mabon Altar

As you have learned early on from this book, Mabon is the celebration of the second part of the harvest. This means that when it comes to food offerings, the best ones to use are those harvested during this period. These may include root crops, squashes, pumpkins, gourds, grapes, potatoes, onions, chili peppers, carrots, red apples, and dried Indian corn. Other nature-themed objects you may include are wreaths made of straw and herbs, acorns, nuts, and leaves in various stages of dryness.

The items listed above are associated with purple, burgundy, crimson, orange, yellow, gold, and other earthy colors. If you can choose the basis of your altar, make sure to use polished wood incorporating these colors. If you have a pre-made surface that looks different from the Mabon color scheme, you can always drape a colored cloth over your altar. Deep brown or red are recommended for larger surfaces as this will be a perfect background for the colors of other items you plan to place on your altar.

If you can only use a small number of tools, such as a few candles, crystals, and symbols, and now harvest produce, use the most colorful pieces of cloth to represent these. For example, you can place a large golden-brown cloth on the altar to symbolize nature and a smaller, purple-colored one on top to represent grapes and red wine. Place a red piece of cloth diagonally across the purple one to illustrate the other fruits of nature.

You will need a centerpiece around which you can place your essential tools and, at the same time, accentuate the down-to-earth feeling you are trying to create with your altar. While a basket made from natural materials would be the best for this purpose, if you only have a plastic bowl at your disposal, use that instead. You can always cover its sides by adorning it with leaves and elements of nature. If you have a small space, you can simply put your offerings inside this bowl or basket. Another idea for a centerpiece would be to use potpourri decorated with tiny scarecrow figures, a common Wiccan practice.

Candles, pillars or taper, and crystals should follow the same color scheme as the other items. They can have a spicy fragrance that reminds you of the season, but if you prefer to use candles without a scent, you can do that too. You can always add more natural scents with ointments if you need specific scents to help you focus. The candles should be placed in a glass jar. This will reflect their light and makes it easier to extinguish them between uses. Light the candles only before casting a spell or performing a ritual, and don't leave them unattended, even if the act needs several hours to complete.

Additional Tips for Setting and Caring for Altars

As you can see, there is a lot to be gained from having a sacred place for your practice and not just for celebrating Mabon. There are also very few rules on how you can or cannot set up an altar for this festivity. As long as you include some of the traditional elements associated with Mabon, you can go on to personalize your space as you like. For newbies, it is generally recommended to have only one main altar in your home as this will allow you to concentrate your power. However, if you are a frequent traveler, you may want to have a mobile altar in addition to the one in your home. Even if you reside in one place, you may not have enough space for an altar in your bedroom. In this case, you can build your main altar elsewhere in the house, and if you would still love to say a dedicated prayer or spell before going to bed, set up a small space for this purpose on your nightstand. Or you may find it helpful to create small shrines in addition to the main altar. The energy will envelop your entire living space, empowering your practice and allowing you to access the power for any purpose from anywhere in your home.

Apart from adorning it with decorations and offerings, there are many other ways to use your altar. In the following chapters, you will find plenty of rituals, spells, and ideas on using your altar in interesting ways during your magical practice, particularly around Mabon. Whichever way you use your altar to celebrate the second harvest, you must not forget to cleanse it regularly. What this cleaning entails depends on how you use the space in the first place. For instance, if you only use it to express your gratitude with a quick prayer, you will only need to cleanse it occasionally. You may need to perform cleanings more frequently if you have a mobile altar. These spaces often come in contact with a larger number of sources of negativity than fixed altars, and you will sense their presence often. In case you plan to make offerings or perform a powerful ritual at your altar during a larger pagan sabbat, you must banish all the negativity from your space first. The purification can be performed in several ways, from smudging to using prayers to calling on spiritual guides.

Chapter 6: Recipes for a Mabon Feast

Mabon is known to be the "Pagan Thanksgiving" by many people. This is why we are here to tell you how to put together the perfect Mabon celebratory feast to enjoy with your friends and family. This chapter serves as a Mabon cookbook that includes delicious seasonal recipes. You will also find a section toward the end of the chapter which will help you understand how you can bless your food with prayers and magic.

Bread is an important part of the feast.
https://unsplash.com/photos/HJ3tXZpY1Qw

Dark Mother: Mabon Honey Wheat Bread

Mabon is an opportunity to celebrate the Dark Mother goddess even in her least comforting forms. This is a time when her presence must be acknowledged, regardless. During Mabon, we celebrate the goddess' wise old woman archetype. There is no better way to do so than by baking a delicious dish that was named in her honor. This appetizing loaf of bread is ideal for celebrating an abundant harvest. You can serve it with Mabon-esque dips like apple butter or herbed oils.

Ingredients:

- Flour: 4 cups

- Flour (whole wheat): 3 cups

- Water: 2 cups

- Honey: 1/3 cup

- Vegetable oil: 1/4 cup

- Butter: 2 tablespoons

- Dry yeast: 1 tablespoon

- Salt: 1 teaspoon

Instructions:

Step One:

1. Take a large bowl and mix the water and yeast. Stir until the yeast is incorporated, and then add the honey.

2. Stir in the vegetable oil, whole wheat flour, and butter. Mix well until you are left with stiff dough,

3. Gradually mix in the all-purpose flour.

4. Lightly flour your countertop before turning your dough out. Knead it for around 15 minutes.

5. The dough should be more malleable and elastic, so you can shape it into a ball.

6. Oil a bowl and place the dough inside. Use a warm, damp cloth to cover it, letting it rise for 45 minutes. It should have doubled in size.

Step Two:

1. Forcefully pat the dough down before you cut it in half, making two loaves of bread.

2. Grease a loaf pan, placing both halves inside. Let them sit and rise.

3. Once they have risen 1 or 2 inches over the loaf pan, move them into the oven.

4. Let them back for an hour at 375 degrees.

5. Remove the bread loaves when they are golden brown and allow them to cool for around 15 minutes.

6. Remove them from the pan and brush them over with melted butter.

Recipe Notes: If you have a bread machine, make sure to halve the number of your ingredients, especially if the machine will do the mixing. The recipe mentioned above makes two loaves of bread.

Spiced Apple Pie

Apple trees, and apples in general, play a significant role in numerous pagan rites, stories, and lore, especially the ones that relate to Samhain and Mabon! Many people place apples on their altars, presenting them as offerings to the deities. They are also used as a way to thank the gods for an abundant harvest. Besides the significance of apples during the Harvest Festival, there is no better way to welcome fall than by baking a warm and comforting spiced apple pie.

Ingredients:

Ingredients for the Crust

- Flour: 1 1/3 cups

- Cubes of unsalted butter (chilled): 1/4 cups

- Frozen solid vegetable shortening (cubed): 1/4 cups

- Ice water: 3 tablespoons

- Salt: 1/2 teaspoon

- Sugar: 1/2 teaspoon

- Apple cider vinegar: 1/2 teaspoon

Ingredients for the Filling

- Sugar: 2/3 cups

- Flour: 2 tablespoons

- Melted unsalted butter: 2 tablespoons

- Ground cinnamon: 2 teaspoons

- Peeled and cored Granny Smith apples (sliced): 3 1/4 pounds

Topping Ingredients

- 1 cup of all-purpose flour

- ½ cup of sugar

- ¼ cup of packed golden-brown sugar

- 6 tbsp of chilled unsalted butter, cut into cubes (around ½ an inch each).

- 1 ½ tsp of ground cinnamon

- ½ tsp of salt

Instructions:

Crust Instructions

Step One:

1. Add the salt, flour, and sugar into a large bowl and mix well.

2. Add the shortening and butter. Make sure to use your fingertips to rub them in until they are coarse.

3. In a small bowl, mix the apple cider vinegar with 3 tbsp of ice water.

4. Drizzle the liquid over the flour mixture. Use a fork to mix well and break down any clumps. If the dough is dry, add more water.

5. Shape the dough into a ball before flattening it out into a circle.

6. Wrap the dough in plastic and leave it to refrigerate for half an hour.

Step Two:

1. Place your oven's rack in the center and preheat at 400 degrees.

2. Lightly flour your countertop, rolling out the dough on top. You should make a 12-inch round.

3. Move the dough to a 9-inch glass pie dish. Cut any excess dough, so there is a slight overhang. Turn the edge underneath the crimp in a decorative manner.

4. Let it refrigerate as you prepare the filling and topping.

Filling Instructions

Step Three:

1. In a large bowl, mix in all the filling ingredients to coat the apples.

Topping Instructions

Step Four:

1. Blend the all-purpose flour, brown sugar, ground cinnamon, and salt in a processor.

2. Use on and off turns (or the pulse function if your processor has one) to cut in the chilled butter cubes. Your mixture should end up looking like wet sand.

Step Five:

1. Toss the filling, making sure that the juices are well distributed.

2. Transfer the filling to the center of the crust.

3. Pack the topping over and surrounding the coated apples.

Preparing the Pie

Step Six:

1. Place the pie on a baking sheet before placing it in the oven.

2. Let it bake for around 40 minutes until the topping turns golden. If the top is becoming golden too quickly, you can use a foil covering to slow it down.

3. Turn down the heat to 350 degrees, allowing the pie to cook for another 45 minutes.

4. Stick a fork into the middle to check that the apples are soft. You should also see the filling start to bubble through the crust.

5. Leave for an hour to cool.

6. Serve with fresh cream or ice cream.

Recipe Notes: This recipe makes eight servings.

Vegetable Pot Pie

Vegetable pot pies are traditionally served during Mabon. This hearty, vegan-friendly recipe is scrumptious and filling and celebrates the essence of the holiday like no other! This is because it incorporates a wide array of seasonal vegetables, allowing you to share the bountiful harvest with everyone you love. As you cook, think of the variety of vegetables that you get to enjoy in a single dish, thanking nature and the deities for this blessing.

Ingredients:

- 8 medium-sized potatoes

- 1 large, finely chopped onion

- 2 9-inch high-quality (preferably whole grain) pie crust.

- 3 cups of your choice of diced vegetables - choose 3 or 4 of the following: broccoli, cauliflower, leeks, carrots, kale, yellow summer squash, mushrooms, zucchini, corn kernels, peas, etc.

- 1 cup of fine whole grain bread crumbs

- 1 cup of home-made or ready-made vegetable stock

- 1/4 cup of minced fresh parsley

- 1/4 cup of nutritional yeast. This is an optional ingredient, but we highly recommend that you use it

- 2 tbsp white flour (unbleached)

- 2 tbsp extra-virgin olive oil

- 1 ½ tbsp of all-purpose seasoning blend

- 1 tsp of dried thyme

- Salt to taste

- Pepper, freshly ground to taste

- Paprika for topping

Instructions:

Step One:

1. Cook the potatoes (or microwave them) in their skins.

2. When they have cooled down a bit, peel them.

3. Dice four of the potatoes and coarsely mash the rest.

4. Set the potatoes aside and preheat the oven to 350 degrees.

Step Two:

1. In a large skillet, heat the oil, and then place the onions. Set fire to medium heat and allow the onions to sauté until they're golden.

2. Mix in the vegetables of your choice. Make sure to add vegetables that require more cooking time, like leeks, broccoli, and cauliflower. Layer the quicker ones on top, such as zucchini, corn, and peas.

3. Add a little water to the pan before covering it. Allow the vegetables to cook for around 5 minutes, so they are tender but *not overcooked.*

Step Three:

1. Sprinkle the flour into the skillet before pouring the stock as well.

2. Mix in the optional nutritional yeast.

3. Cook for one or two more minutes, stirring until the liquid becomes thicker.

4. Add the diced and mashed potatoes, mixing them in well.

5. Stir in the thyme, parsley, and seasoning blend, then add salt and freshly ground pepper to taste.

6. Once done, place the mixture inside the pie crusts, patting it in well.

7. Sprinkle the bread crumbs over both pies, distributing them evenly. Finish off with a sprinkle of paprika over each.

8. Place in the preheated oven and allow them to bake for 35 to 40 minutes.

9. Remove the pies when the crust is golden, allowing them to sit at room temperature for around 10 minutes.

10. Cut into wedges and serve.

Recipe Notes: This recipe makes two pies and around 12 servings in total.

Mabon Roasted Turkey

As you already know, Mabon and Thanksgiving go almost hand in hand. While Thanksgiving is a national holiday, both celebrations are centered on the idea of giving thanks.

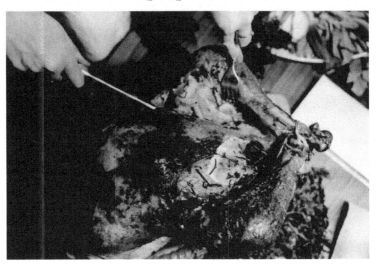

Roast turkey.
https://unsplash.com/photos/cgctcFH-azk

They are also associated with the end of the harvesting season. While there is no symbolic reason as to why turkeys are served on either holiday, it is a tradition that has stood for generations. Perhaps one of the reasons why turkeys are preferred over, say, chicken, on celebrations like Mabon, Thanksgiving, or even Christmas, is that they are large enough to sustain a feast. The following roasted turkey recipe will surely make your Mabon celebration a memorable one.

Ingredients:

- 1 thawed whole turkey (9 pounds)
- 1 medium-sized red onion cut in quarters
- 1 lemon cut in quarters
- ¼ cup of olive oil

- 1 tbsp of dried rosemary

- 1 tsp of dried thyme

- 1 tsp fine sea salt

- 1 tsp of dried tarragon

- ½ tsp of black pepper, freshly ground

Instructions:

Step One:

1. Set the temperature of the roaster oven to 325 degrees to preheat.

2. In a small bowl, start making the herbal rub by mixing in the olive oil, tarragon, rosemary, thyme, pepper, and salt.

3. Remove the neck and the giblets from the turkey. If you are making stock or gravy, you can use the neck and giblets to make them.

4. Use cold water to wash the turkey, then pat it dry.

5. Loosen, but don't remove it from the breast using your fingertips. Spread a tablespoon's worth of herbal rub on the meat below the loosened skin.

6. Spread more of the rub on the meat at the neck and body cavities.

7. Spread the rest of the rub on the skin outside the turkey.

Step Two:

1. Quarter the lemon and onion and stuff them into the body and neck cavities. In most cases, you will be able to fit one lemon quarter in the neck cavity, and the rest will be stuffed in the body.

2. Use toothpicks to secure the neck skin at the back. Fold the turkey's wing tips underneath its back and bind its legs in place.

3. If you wish, you can pause at this point and store it in the refrigerator for a few hours.

Step Three:

1. The turkey should be placed back down on the tray or rack. Lower it into the roaster and place a meat thermometer on its thigh. Make sure to stick it into the thickest part, steering clear of the bones.

2. Leave the turkey to roast in the preheated oven for around 2.5 hours. As a rule of thumb, each pound of turkey should take 15 to 20 minutes to roast.

3. Baste the turkey every half an hour. If you do not start out with enough pan juices, add one or two tablespoons of olive oil.

4. When the turkey turns your desired shade of brown, use aluminum foil to create a loose tent to cover it with. This will help you avoid over-browning. Lift it up when it is time to baste.

5. Allow the turkey to roast until the meat thermometer reads 165 degrees.

Step Four:

1. Turn the roaster off and remove the lid.

2. Allow the turkey to rest for 5 minutes before lifting the turkey using the rack from the oven.

3. Place the rack with the turkey on a platter, leaving it to rest for an additional 10 minutes.

4. Remove the rack and carve the turkey on your platter.

Recipe Notes: This roasted turkey recipe makes around ten servings. It works well with a small to medium-sized turkey (follow the 15 to 20-minute per pound rule). 1 pound of a whole turkey should feed a bit over one person.

Keep in mind that turkey meat is easy to dry out. This is why you should not skip over the olive oil and the frequent basting.

If you wish to stuff the turkey, avoid bread or grain-based savory stuffing, as they can hinder the cooking process. Instead, choose juicy vegetable and fruit stuffing instead. These provide flavor and moisture and may even be discarded later. You can add savory stuffing in the cavity right before you serve the turkey.

Winter Squash with Peas and Mashed Potatoes Stuffing

If you are not a carnivore, or if you have many vegan guests coming over, this is yet another vegetable-based delectable meal to keep everyone satisfied. This recipe uses seasonal ingredients like squash and potatoes, getting right to the essence of the celebration.

Ingredients:

- 6 medium-sized potatoes. They should be peeled and diced.

- 2 medium-sized squash - butternut or carnival. Each should weigh around 1.5 to 2 pounds.

- 1 large carrot cut into thick, 2-inch-long sticks

- 1 large onion chopped

- 1 cup of frozen petite green peas thawed

- ½ cup of rice milk

- 1 tbsp of olive oil. You can use an alternative vegetable oil of your choice

- 2 tsp of salt-free seasoning blend

- Nutmeg - a pinch

- Salt to taste

- Pepper, freshly ground to taste

Instructions:

Step One:

1. Preheat the oven to 400 degrees.

2. Cut the squash in half - vertically. Remove all the fibers and seeds.

3. Line a shallow baking pan with foil.

4. Cover the squash with aluminum foil, placing both cut halves, side up, in the lined baking pan.

5. Allow them to bake for 4o to 50 minutes. They should be firm yet easily pierced with a knife.

6. Remove when done and allow them to cool down.

7. Use a spoon to scoop out the pulp. You should have around a ¼ or ½-inch of firm shell all around.

8. Mash the pulp and set it aside.

Step Two:

1. Place the potatoes in a large saucepan and cover it with enough water.

2. Bring the saucepan to a simmer. Cover it and let it simmer steadily for around 10 to 15 minutes or until the potatoes are tender.

Step Three:

1. Heat the oil in a medium-sized skillet as you wait for the potatoes to cook.

2. Add the carrot and onion to the skillet to sauté them. Remove them when the carrot is crisp yet tender and the onion is golden.

Step Four:

1. When the potatoes are cooked, drain the potatoes and place them in a mixing bowl.

2. Pour in the rice milk and mash the potatoes until they're smooth.

3. Add the onions and carrots and mix well.

4. Stir in the ginger, peas, and nutmeg, followed by the squash pulp from earlier.

5. Mix gently, so everything is well-integrated into the mashed potatoes.

Step Five:

1. Distribute the mixture among the four squash shells.

2. Bake for 15 minutes.

3. Serve each half as a large portion or cut each half horizontally to make eight smaller portions

Recipe Notes: This recipe makes four large portions. If this is not one of your main dishes, you can cut each squash half into half to create eight small portions to make a great side dish.

Homemade Chai Tea

Nothing embodies the spirit of fall like chai tea! The comforting, warming, and relaxing combination of seasonal spices, milk, and black tea makes the ideal Mabon beverage. Serve this aromatic drink to your guests after dinner for a full celebratory experience. Not only is chai tea flavorful, but it can also aid with digestion and help them unwind after a busy day.

Ingredients:

- Black tea: 5-8 bags
- 2 sticks of cinnamon
- One knob of ginger, thinly cut
- 6 pods of cardamom
- 10 cloves
- Cold water: 6 cups
- Whole milk: 2 cups
- Golden brown sugar: 1/2 cup
- Black pepper: 2 teaspoons

Instructions:

Step One:

1. Add the spices and pepper to a large pan.
2. Muddle the spices together, crushing and grinding them with a wooden spoon.

Step Two:

1. Add the water and bring the mixture to a boil.
2. Reduce the heat and simmer for 8-12 minutes.
3. Add in the tea and allow to simmer for 4 minutes.
4. Strain the mixture.

Step Three:

1. Add sugar and milk to taste.

2. Continue to monitor the heat and simmer the mixture, stirring to incorporate the sugar.

3. Serve the tea.

Recipe Note: This recipe serves six people.

How to Imbue Your Food with Magic

People have used prayers, magic, blessings, and grace for centuries to imbue their food with magical powers. Numerous cultures have their own special ways of making food sacred. If you think about it, each religion comes with its own eating rituals, which involve practitioners saying blessings over their food. The primary intention behind this practice is to express thankfulness and gratitude for having something to eat.

Saying grace, however, can be tied to much more than being thankful. Grace is the feeling of joy that you get whenever you replenish your body after being hungry. In a sense, grace resonates with "salvation" more than it does with thankfulness. If you have tried fasting, then the chances are that you can resonate with this feeling.

Not only is food a blessing and essential to life, but it also requires sacrifices to be made. Whether you are eating meat or a vegetable, something has to die so you can have food on your plate. This is why you should thank the Earth and god for it.

There are several things you can do to bless your food. You can say a prayer of grace over your meal or practice invocation and other types of magic.

Theophagy

You can practice theophagy as a method of imbuement by combining visualization with the physical interaction with food (cooking and ingestion). Theophagy is essentially a ritualistic practice where food or drinks are substituted with the body of a god. These substitutes can be grains, vegetables, entheogens, animals, etc. Since no one can get hold of a physical object that relates to a god, you can imbue your food with the name or qualities of your desired god while you are cooking it or before you ingest it.

Grow Your Awareness

Did you know that our digestion is affected by our mood and mental state? If you eat when you are angry, for instance, this can negatively impact your ability to digest food. Performing rituals and saying grace can help us clear our energies and balance our emotions, which would then allow us to benefit from the food that we are eating. Bring your awareness to your emotions while you eat. Try to be sincerely thankful, joyful, and grateful throughout the entire experience.

Say Prayers

Bless your feast with the following prayer before you eat:

"In this sacred time and place,

we celebrate the balance of the equinox

around our community feast table.

We've set a bountiful feast, for which we are thankful.

We enjoy many blessings of our harvests this turning,

and we receive them with humility and gratitude.

May this food and drink nourish our bodies,

and this assembly of friends nourishes our hearts

so that we may be strengthened for our journey into the coming dark.

At this time of our bounty, we remember times of lack.

We remember that life gives itself in sacrifice so that others may live,

Knowing there are those who are suffering,

we hold them in the light of Divine love, and we offer a pledge to give of ourselves as we are able

in service for a greater harvest.

May the blessings of Spirit flow through us.

We are love and light, sacrifice and shadow,

toil and harvest. We are complete.

For all that is lost, there is gain.

When all is lost, we look to hope.

When our hearts ache, we still have happiness.

I can only rise again if I first fall.

But give me not too much of any one thing.

May we remain ever mindful, in deepest gratitude.

Blessed be."

Now that you have read this chapter, you are ready to prepare and plan a Mabon feast. The recipes above will guarantee a memorable second harvest feast. Imbuing your food with one of the spiritual essences we have explained can help you further incorporate the magic of the holiday into the cooking and feasting experience.

Chapter 7: Family and Group Activities

Festivals and holidays are meant to be commemorated with friends and families, and Mabon is no different. As Mabon is a festival that revolves around harvest and history tells us that pagans and Celts used to celebrate this day to thank Mother Nature for a good harvest.

So, when celebrating Mabon, your plans should also swirl around nature, harvest, and promote natural resources.

Moreover, one of the main reasons behind celebrating this day is to pray for the yield to last throughout the winter season. Therefore, as a follower and believer, you have to nurture this idea in younger generations to keep them in touch with the holy tradition of Mabon.

To celebrate the real essence of this festival, you must plan activities accordingly to make the day interesting and enjoyable for your family and maintain its educational aspect.

And to help you with the planning group and family activities during this festive season, we are sharing some tips in this chapter to help to make it a memorable time for you and the people closest to you.

Planning a Mabon Feast

Mabon is a holy festival and carries a lot of significance for all pagan believers. As a matter of fact, Mabon shares a lot of similarities with Thanksgiving.

Interestingly, the concept behind Mabon, as well as Thanksgiving, is to celebrate the harvesting season. Therefore, the meals usually made in a Mabon feast are symbolic, too, much like we have in our Thanksgiving dinners.

Some foods symbolic of the Mabon feast are nuts, pomegranates, bread, mutton, goose, and carrots.

Tips for Organizing a Mabon Dinner/Feast

Mabon is a big and hearty dinner with several guests. It is imperative to plan it well beforehand to avoid any inconvenience on the day. Also, it is a must to assess your budget while planning so that the expenses will not get out of your hand during preparations. Keeping that in mind, here are some tips to help you with the arrangements for the Mabon dinner.

1. Use of Mother Nature

The common theme of all rituals and festivities concerning Mabon is to respect Mother Nature, so arranging a nature-friendly themed dinner is appropriate. Use natural resources to decorate the area and create a Mabon altar. It is also better to keep your meals season-friendly by using fresh vegetables and fruits. Some of the most common things you can get your hands on during the festival days include walnuts, hazelnuts, berries, mushrooms, corn husks, pinecones, and seasonal vegetables.

2. When to Hold the Mabon Feast

In most countries, the festival comes right at the beginning of the school year, and it will be nearly impossible for most families to hold a huge celebration every year, especially if it does not fall on the weekend. But it does not mean you cannot celebrate the festival.

The best way to celebrate Mabon with your family is by holding a family meal at the end of the day. In that case, arrange a delightful yet simple dinner, put bouquets of fresh flowers or candles on the dinner table, and give each family member a chance to let out their thoughts about things they are grateful for and what they want to achieve in the coming season.

3.   Plan Every Detail

In normal circumstances, a Mabon feast would be a huge gathering comprising family members, friends, and relatives, and to organize a dinner of that scale, you have to be spot on with every little detail while planning.

4.   How to Plan a Menu

First, make a list of the guests and send them invites. Once you know the number of guests, it will help you keep a count of the preparations. The second and one of the most important things is to plan a menu. Always consider the dietary priorities of your guest before finalizing the menu. It is better to arrange both veg and non-veg options for varied preferences. Add a dessert, too, because a sweet delicacy is a wonderful way of wrapping up things. Arrange a handful of drinks, too, because no matter what you put on the menu to eat, drinks can enhance the whole feel of the menu.

5.   Organize the Spot

The thing you just cannot do is overlook the place where the actual dinner is going to take place. The dinner arena should be cleaned a day before the festival. Make sure your place is decorated according to the selected theme, and the dishes are done beforehand. It is always a great idea to decorate the entrance with fresh flowers and traditional autumn greenery. Another thing to ensure as a host is to arrange enough garbage bags so that the actual dinner place will stay tidy the whole day of the festival.

6. What to Avoid

Now that we have discussed everything that needs to be done in order to make your Mabon feast a hit, it is time to point out some of the chores that should be avoided to prevent any inconvenience on the prestigious occasion.

- Never make a mistake by inviting guests to dinner before making a manageable plan. For a special dinner, you must make a well-versed plan at least a month before the day of the festival.

- Understandably, you would want to invite everyone you know in your circle to this day, but it is imperative, too, that you think realistically about your budget, time, and the spot of the dinner.

- As we have discussed earlier, it is a must to consider the guests' dietary preferences while finalizing the menu. Try to prepare a multidimensional menu that includes vegetarian and non-veg meals to accommodate guests with different dietary preferences and needs.

- Do not forget to arrange enough cutlery, plates, pots, pans, and forks according to the decided menu to avoid any inconvenience during the dinner.

- The quantity of food is one the most important part to consider while planning. It is the part where people often miscalculate things, and it will eventually become the reason for embarrassment for the host. Also, you do not want to send your guests home starving on the Mabon feast.

- As with the food, always calculate the number of drinks you are going to need for the day. Always arrange some spare bottles just in case. A common mistake you would want to avoid is to arrange only alcoholic drinks. A bottle of wine is good, but it is imperative to arrange a handful of non-alcoholic drinks too for people who do not like or want to drink alcohol.

- Another big mistake people make is becoming a control freak and doing everything on their own, which generally takes a toll on their health physically and mentally. As a result, they do not get to enjoy the actual event at the expense of preparation. So, it is always good to ask for assistance and bring some help in the kitchen to ensure everything goes smoothly.

- I am not sure why, but many people make the mistake of trying new recipes out on that day, and it is always a risk and must be avoided at any cost. Suppose you have found some new exciting Mabon feast recipes and are itching to cook them at the festival. In that case, it is better to try those recipes beforehand to ensure everything turns out well to avoid any inconvenience (or embarrassment) in front of your guests.

- Cooking leaves a handful of dirty pans, pots, and utensils, and it is always a good idea to do to wash them up as you go. It will eventually save you a lot of time and hassle at the end of the day.

- Obviously, the main activity in a Mabon feast must be eating, but you cannot ignore the fact that if you do not have anything else planned besides dinner, your guests will be bored. To avoid that, arrange some fun activities for the children, turn the TV on for sports lovers, or engage your guests in some fun party games, all while they wait for the food to be served.

- Another thing you can do is arrange regular snacks for your guests to keep everyone tidy and fresh until dinner is served.

- Lastly: people often tend to forget the main idea behind the Mabon dinner – to enjoy and celebrate with friends and family. So, it is imperative that the host must take some time out of the preparatory hustles of the kitchen and enjoy the moment.

An alternative to a Potluck Mabon Dinner

For some people, hosting a Potluck Mabon dinner is not really possible for many reasons. But that doesn't mean that if you cannot hold a Mabon dinner, you cannot celebrate the festival at all. There are many other ways to celebrate and enjoy the festivity with your family, and this section is all about that.

1. Bring All the Apples

Apple is the most prominent symbol of the Mabon festival. You don't need to go all out with your feast at this time of year; even just consuming apples (in their various forms) will suffice.

2. Built Your Very Own Mabon Altar

This is the most satisfying thing to do at the Mabon festival. An altar represents a significant portion of the spiritual aspect of a Pagan. Creating an altar in your home on this prestigious occasion is a form of celebration in itself. The Mabon altar is created for numerous reasons, to pray, cast spells or hold ceremonies.

You can build your Mabon altar anywhere you want or have space in your home. Be sure to incorporate the four elements into your altar, symbolizing fire, water, air, and earth in different ways. You can also include something representing your faith, e.g., a goddess candle or a book of shadows.

Another major element that you can add to a Mabon altar is seasonal and ceremonial symbols and colors. Mabon is usually represented with fall colors like brown, gold, and orange. Hence, Mabon is a festival to celebrate the harvest. You can also add symbols to represent the seasonal harvest, including apples, wheat, pomegranate, corn, pumpkin, and other seasonal vegetables.

3. Mabon Balance Meditation

As Mabon is that time of the year when, for a short period, day and night appear to be of the same length of time, or, as it is referred to by the ancient pagans, the periods of light and dark come into balance. Pagans widely believe that the energy of the planet is ideal for meditating and seeking balance in our own lives too.

You will need a black and white candle and a place devoid of stress, confusion, and clutter. Light both candles and close your eyes to begin entry into your meditative state. Breathe in and out while focusing on your breathing, and think about what you need help with in your life. Now right after that, turn your focus on things that are more or less a reason for your happiness or goals that you want to achieve in your life in the near future.

Now the most important part, it is time to acknowledge the blessings of god and understand that with every negative, there is a positive too that comes side by side.

4. Connect with Mother Nature

As we have discussed in the earlier part of the chapter, the real idea behind all of this is to celebrate the harvest and thank god for its countless blessings. Besides all those rituals and indoor festivities, the best way to celebrate it is to connect with nature. You can do that in many ways depending on the time, resources available, and the commitment you would like to give. Whatever you plan, encourage your family to take part in these healthy activities too.

For starters, it is easier to go for a walk at any nearby park or go hiking on trails located in your vicinity with your family. If you can commit, pack up and go camping or sleep with the stars – one of the most amazing things you can do to appreciate and celebrate nature. If you have small children, teach them to appreciate and respect the blessings of the environment.

Various Mabon Activities to Indulge in

Let us discuss some other Mabon activities you can indulge in on the day besides those we have talked about up until now. In this section, we will focus on those activities that can be adapted by the

Pagans, especially Wiccans and Druids.

1. Mindful Autumn Cleaning

Mabon is when the balance of light and dark shifts towards the other side of the horizon, and the planet earth experiences a change in temperatures. It is considered an ideal time to clean and organize your home.

Take the negative energies out of your home by decluttering, and put some effort into completing any outstanding repairing work on your home. After you are done with physical cleaning, it is time to move your focus toward the spiritual side of it. This is considered the most important part of this activity, and pagans usually go through a candle ritual that involves several traditional rituals, charging protection, ritual smudging, and healing crystals. Adopt any one of these rituals by following your heart.

2. Extend Your Blessings to Others

Besides following the central concept of the Mabon festival, which is to thank and pray to god for the harvest and blessings, it is also a time when you should reach out to the less blessed people or the ones struggling to make both ends meet. You can do that by sticking to the basic symbol of the festival, harvest, holding a food drive for deserving people, and encouraging others to do the same.

In case you are not in a position to help others financially, it is ok, as most of us have gone through that phase too. In that case, if you can keep your positive energy going, you can physically participate in that holy cause by working for food banks organized by others. The idea is to keep your mind fresh with positive energies.

3. Planting Bulb Flowers

One fun and positive activity that you can indulge in is planting. And this is the ultimate time of the year to plant different tree seeds, especially bulb flowers. They usually hide in the earth throughout the winter, which helps them stabilize and germinate in darkness until the spring arrives, when you will see your planted seeds germinate and appear on the surface.

4. Write a Gratitude Journal

If you have a collection of those beautiful little notebooks you have never bothered to touch after bringing them home years ago, this is the time to use them for good. Gather all your positive thoughts about the things that happen to you and which you feel good about, and write them in that notebook. It will make you feel better about yourself and your surroundings. Plus, it will work as a signal to the earthly heavens that you need those moments to happen more often in your life in the future.

5. Host a Bonfire

A tradition not really original to the Mabon festival but recognized worldwide and throughout known history is that harvest festivals are meant to end on that very activity, burning a fire. So, it is a no-brainer to arrange something traditional that also has significance in the history books. Invite your friends, loved ones, and other closely related people and set the scene in the environment. Be sure to burn all those things that are not good for you and your loved ones, tell stories, listen to other people, and raise a toast for everyone's safety and health.

Kid-Friendly Mabon Activities

Mabon is the festival meant to unite us with our families, loved ones, and friends, and we are meant to thank Mother Nature for her blessings upon us. And our kids certainly are an integral part of the blessings of God upon us. So, if you are lucky enough to have those little munchkins at your home, involve them in this prestigious occasion and arrange some interesting and enjoyable activities to make them feel better about this holy festival. And if you cannot think of one, here are some fun activities you can arrange for your kids to indulge in.

- To create a Mabon altar, you will need a handful of natural resources such as acorns, nuts, apples, seasonal vegetables, colorful flowers or leaves, ivy, and other natural items you think your kids will love. It would be great for your children if you could take them out and handpick these items so that your children can appreciate the beauty and blessings of nature.

- You can start the festival by making a flavorful apple pie in the morning. Try to engage your children in the baking process too. It will help them grow as human beings and make them appreciative of you and other fellow humans.

- If you are holding a Mabon feast at home, keep the children busy with some fun games and activities. A healthy activity you can organize for them is to engage them in creating paper bouquets, especially autumn flowers.

- Show your kids the old family albums and answer their questions. Also, tell them the stories behind those pictures and tell them about the people and legacy they left behind respectfully.

- You can also honor the wildlife in your vicinity by making bird feeders and inspiring your children to do the same in the coming years.

- Keep a close eye on your family habits and try to find the appropriate solutions to those manners that you feel are inappropriate for the environment and your fellow human beings. For example, use less water, do not waste food, keep a light tone while conversing or recycle more garbage. Your children will learn a lot, making them better people altogether.

- Read stories to them about harvest, Autumn season, and Mabon. It will educate them and give them the whole idea behind the celebration.

- Arrange a question-and-answer session for children so they can ask whatever they have in their minds about the festival, traditions, and religious practices of Pagans.

Chapter 8: Sacred Rituals and Ceremonies

Traditional rituals and ceremonies related to Mabon revolve around celebrating abundance and being thankful. However, many other ways to celebrate the fall equinox include inward reflection, forming spiritual connections, or planning for what you will plant next year. This chapter includes several rituals and ceremonies you can incorporate into your Mabon celebrations. Some of them are more suitable for groups. Others can be performed by solo practitioners and will take only a few minutes of your day.

Mabon Meditation

Mabon is the ideal time of the year to release any negative emotions you carry on your shoulders and harvest some positive ones instead. Meditative practice can help you do this and will not take much time from your schedule either.

Many crops are harvested during Mabon, but at the same time, you cannot help but notice the first signs of nature dying as it prepares for the harsh winter months. The equinox represents a unique balance between the bright side of the year that is now ending and the dark side that is yet to come. Day and night are of equal lengths, another sign of natural balance. It reminds you that you cannot expect the light to come out the following year without experiencing darkness in this one.

Ideally, you should meditate in the evening and preferably outside, as this will give you a stronger connection with the spirits of nature. You can also do it at an altar you have set up inside your home. Here is how to perform a Mabon meditation, regardless of the place you have chosen for it:

- Decorate your altar or an outside flat surface with leaves, acorns, nuts, small amounts of fruit and vegetables, and other autumn symbols mentioned in this book.

- Place a black and a white candle at the center of your working area, and light them both.

- Sit comfortably, take a deep breath, and close your eyes so that you can start to relax.

- Now recall everything you have been struggling with lately and everything that caused you harm or made you anxious.

- Repeat the following:

  "I seek the balance of day and night,

  brought on by this Mabon night

  I seek balance in my life

  as it is found in nature.

  The back candle is illuminated because we all have to suffer at times.

  and the candle will help to remove my suffering.

  The white candle is illuminated for the happiness in my life

  and all that will come my way as I dedicate my life.

  This is Mabon when the light and dark are equal,

  and the balance transcends my soul and brings inner peace,

  and the harmony shall continue within me."

- Continue meditating on everything you wish to change in your life, leaving hurtful memories behind.

- When you feel cleansed from negative energy, start invoking abundance and positivity into your life.

- Open yourself to receiving every spiritual gift possible, and be prepared to express your gratitude for them.

- Let the scent of the burning candles permeate your senses, carrying renewed energy and purpose with it.

- Accept that there are and always will be challenging times in life, and embracing them is the only way to move past them.

- Once you can finally embrace the balance of light and dark, you will be ready to finish your session with a deep exhalation.

- Bring the present back to your mind's focus, stand up, extinguish your candles, and go to sleep.

Dark Mother Ritual

This ritual celebrates all Dark Mothers, and, as such, can be personally tailored depending on which entity you feel spiritually connected to. Inanna, Demeter, Hecate, Tiamet, Nemesis, Kali, and Morrighan are just some of the female deities you can evoke, one or more of them at a time. The Dark Mother is an aspect of goddesses that you may not find too appealing, but its existence is essential for balancing the more comforting aspects. By acknowledging the Dark Mother with this ritual, you are repeating and honoring an ancient tradition of creating an energetic balance for healing from past traumas.

You Will Need:

- Symbols of a pagan goddess known to have a dark side

- Red, yellow, purple, and black flowers

- A basket full of wheat, Indian corn, and other crops representing the second harvest

- A black candle

- A yellow or red candle

- A cup of wine or juice from a red fruit

- A pomegranate

- A bowl, a knife, and a spoon

Instructions:

1. Place all of your items on your altar and perform your usual preparatory practices. Whether you call to cast a circle, call on your spiritual guides, meditate or perform any other mindfulness exercise, it will be up to you.

2. After that, turn back to the altar, light the dark candle, and recite the following:

   "As the land begins to die, and the earth grows cold.

   What once brought life does not anymore.

   As the Dark Mother comes to harvest,

   So does nature continue its descent into night.

   As we mourn the death of nature

   We also mourn the long daylight

   and prepare for winter as it approaches us."

3. The yellow/red candle can be illuminated, incanting:

   "Anger and pain bring the Dark Mother to the world.

   The harvest shall wither as the time of change becomes upon us.

   She travels around us looking for the bounty,

   forgoing darkness as the crops meet their end.

   We share in the grief that she takes on for us,

   And we hope she finds the light that she will bring to us.

We cannot have the light without the darkness."

4. Cut the pomegranate and remove six of the seeds, placing them in your receptacle. Place on the altar and incant:

   "Six months of light can only follow six months of darkness.

   We rise back to life only after death has touched us.

   Great Mabon, let this be your night,

   And let us celebrate it with you.

   We embrace the darkness,

   And celebrate the life of the Crone.

   Blessings to the dark goddess on this night."

5. Lift the cup of wine or juice from the altar and place it back and hold your hand out as if you would reach for the goddess.

6. Reflect on the darker aspects of your life, including the pain you are carrying from past traumas, any anger or frustration still worrying you, and unsaid grievances towards others.

7. Now, focus on turning all this negativity into positivity by saying the following:

   "Bringer of darkness,

   I am ready to embrace you tonight.

   What is love without first experiencing loss and grief,

   What is joy without knowing pain,

   What is light without the dark,

   and what is life without first death?

   O Dark Mother of the night, I thank you."

8. When you are ready to accept every aspect of your soul, you may end the ritual and extinguish your candles. Leave the wine and other offerings out for the goddess.

Mabon Gratitude Ritual

This short gratitude ritual incorporates elements you and your group can use to express your gratitude for everything you have. You can also perform it by yourself, although it holds even more power if a tight-knit pagan community performs it during Mabon night. It can be incorporated into other traditions or beliefs or, kept as it is, a short pagan rite for giving thanks. It includes symbols of those aspects of your life that you are grateful to have.

You Will Need:

- Gold or green candle to represent abundance. The number of colors you need depends on the number of participants

- Basket of apples or grapes

- 1/8 cup of neutral oil of your choice

- 5 drops of rose oil

- 2 drops of vetiver oil

- 1 drop of agrimony oil

- A pinch of ground cinnamon

- Cornucopias as the symbol of bounty

- An abundance symbol (preferably hand crafted)

- Representations of things you are grateful for (health, career, family, etc.)

- Pieces of cloth or craft material in colors associated with abundance

Instructions:

1. If you do not have it already prepared, make your oil blend by mixing all the oils with the cinnamon.

2. Start decorating your altar with all the items by placing your fruit basket in the middle. Then put the symbols in front and the two candles on either side of the basket. Scatter the

other items and colorful pieces of material around the larger centerpiece.

3. Gather around before going to sleep, let everyone take a deep breath, and close their eyes.

4. Take a moment to consider what you have in abundance. Keep in mind that means much more than having plenty of material goods or a high income.

5. Think about friends and family ties, even with those who have already passed away. You can be thankful for all the wisdom the ancestors provided during their life and even after that.

6. If you have a trusty spiritual guide you use regularly, you may include them in your intention for saying thanks.

7. Everyone should anoint a candle with the oil mixture and light it.

8. One by one, each participant can express their gratitude. Start at one corner of the altar and slowly work towards the other one until everyone has said their thanks.

9. Here are some ideas on what to say:

   "I am thankful for my health because it makes me feel well.

   I am grateful to my children because their love keeps me happy.

   I appreciate my job because I can do what I love while having financial independence.

   My garden fills me with joy for the abundance of food and medicine it brings.

   I am grateful for my friends and family because they make me feel complete."

10. Let everyone meditate for five minutes after the last person has expressed their gratitude out loud.

11. If you are conducting this ritual as a group, the members can also express their appreciation for each other. If you are a solitary practitioner, you can call or message people you

appreciate having in your life. There is always a way to let them know how much their presence means to you; it is just a question of taking the time for it.

Group Apple Picking at Mabon

The best part about large pagan holidays is that they always unite communities. Whether you and your loved ones share the same spiritual beliefs or not, everyone will find their fill of joy and happiness, particularly during this ritual. It involves picking apples as a group and strictly as a group, with a side of gratitude. After pumpkins, apples are probably the most commonly harvested fall fruit. In pagan communities, apples are grown for several purposes, but group pickings are among the most important. Gathering apples with your loved ones is one of the best ways to appreciate the gifts of nature.

You only need apples and perhaps comfortable clothing for this ritual.

Instructions:

1. Gather people from your community, go to the nearest apple orchards and pick as many apples as possible.

2. After harvesting the apples, gather around and sit on the ground in a circle. If the weather is getting colder, you can all converge inside and sit on the floor.

3. Hold an apple in your hands and start expressing your gratitude. Each person should have a few minutes to say what or whom they appreciate most in life.

4. When the last person in the circle has said their thanks, get up and continue with your Mabon celebration.

Group Expeditions

Another way pagans can express their gratitude as a group around the fall equinox is by going on short expeditions in nature. You can go hiking or for a walk, whatever the group decides, and observe nature around you. Make sure to notice all the changes in the landscape and acknowledge the necessity for these changes. You can also repeat this at the spring equinox and compare the transformation you see then with the one you experience before winter.

Your group can also visit a farmer's market or a farm where you can buy fresh organic produce. Everyone can choose a unique ingredient to take home and add it to a celebratory meal you all make together. This can be a fun activity for children as they can learn more about natural food sources while bonding with their family members.

Making Donations

Just as they do at any other festivity, people in pagan communities are famous for sharing what they have with those in need. If you live in such a community and practice together as a group, all of you can gather food and supplies you can donate. However, solitary practitioners are just as welcome to inspire others with their generosity. There is no better way to express gratitude for the abundance of anything you have in your life than by sharing it with the less fortunate.

Morning Gratitude Ritual

While most people express their gratitude on the night of the equinox, there is no reason that you could not do this for several days leading up to this date. The best way to do it is to begin your days with a ritual of appreciation. Start bright and early on the first morning of the Mabon celebrations. Write three to five things you are grateful for on a piece of paper. You can write more if you can think of them immediately, but do not worry if you can only come up with three at first. Create your crafts and recipes, and start decorating your altar to get inspired and find more things to be grateful for. You will soon start adding more and more items to your lists and by the night of the equinox comes, your list will be rather long.

Autumn Cleansing Ritual

While most people get inspired to clean their homes in spring, fall can be just as great a time to catch up on some much-needed chores. And, yes, even chores can be a Mabon ritual. You can perform spiritual and energetic cleansing by smudging your place. Or you can literally dust and air out your home preparing it for the bounty of the harvest and some positive energy you'll need during the cold winter months.

Solitary Grounding Ritual

While you can explore nature around you in a group, conducting a solitary grounding ritual is a good idea to form an even stronger bond with nature. Performing it in solitude will allow you to connect directly to the vital energy. It will also provide a place to feel safe during a transition period such as the fall equinox. By placing your feet on the ground, you can feel how the energy travels from the earth, enters your legs and travels upward through the rest of your body.

Mabon Ritual for Good Harvests and Other Rewards Ahead

Like a Mabon meditation session, this ritual also has the purpose of balancing the dark with light. It is the perfect way to ensure that the second harvest will be just as bountiful as the first one and that you will receive spiritual rewards in other parts of your life.

You Will Need:

- A white or clear crystal to represent light

- A dark gemstone to represent the dark

- A white candle that symbolizes the light side of harvest (the bounty)

- A black candle that symbolizes the dark side of harvest (dying nature)

- White sage, copal, and other herbs for smudging

- Your favorite essential oil or natural perfume

Instructions:

1. Place the light tools on the left side of your altar and the dark tools on the right side. Keeping them apart is crucial before you cleanse them to avoid mixing energies.

2. Keep the essential oil in the middle for now.

3. Create a smudge stick from your herbs, light them, and use them to cleanse the rest of the items. Start the smudging with the lighter items and slowly move on to the darker ones.

4. Take a deep breath as you inhale the smoke created by the smudging stick and try to sense the energy of each tool you have on your altar.

5. If you have trouble deciding how to start integrating your tools into one balanced whole, call upon your spirit guides to find out how to approach this process.

6. When you feel that one of the candles is ready to be moved, pick it up and place it beside the stones on the opposite side. Shortly afterward, you can move the other candle and light them both.

7. As you see the light candle shining over the dark stones and the dark one over the light crystals, you will feel a balance forming between light and shadow.

8. Enjoy the liberating experience mixing sides brings. Start embracing it and continue mixing and matching by rearranging the stones until you feel that a balance has been fully established.

9. Step back and gaze at the play of light and dark. Consider the lessons you can learn from this experience while you breathe deeply.

10. At this point, you may receive messages from your spiritual guides to make sure to keep an open mind about them.

11. Bring your hands forward in a prayer position in front of your heart and express your gratitude for everything you have achieved and learned.

12. At this moment of balance, welcome whatever the future may still hold and promise to integrate it into your life, whether there are good or bad experiences.

Finding the Right Mabon Traditions for You

As you can see, there are many ways to celebrate Mabon. Practices can be based on things like your spiritual beliefs, the number of people celebrating, or the flora and fauna you have available where you live. Feel free to use the rituals and ceremonies discussed in this chapter, but do not forget to add your own twist to them. By listening to your intuition, you can make your Mabon celebration as simple or complicated as you want them to be.

If you prefer to express your gratitude alone, choose simple rituals focusing on spiritual opening and development. On the other hand, if you are open to social celebrations, you can invite fellow practitioners and even non-pagan friends and family members to join you. Everyone shares the fun during Mabon, from cleaning to gathering supplies to enjoying delicious feasts.

Chapter 9: Spells, Charms, and Baths

Mabon can also be celebrated with different spells, baths, and even by creating your own harvest charms. This chapter brings you plenty of spells to enact centered on the second harvest, with user-friendly instructions on how and when to say them. Most of them use harvest-related ingredients presented in the previous chapters and can be tied to rituals, prayer, or meditative practices suitable for this spell. As expected, Mabon spells are all about celebrating abundance, expressing gratitude, and preparing to transition from summer to winter.

Healing Apple Magic

As apples are one of the most plentiful products around Mabon time, they are often used in spells and rituals as symbols of abundance and something to be thankful for. However, this same quality makes apples perfect for healing magic spells. As you reflect on what you need to be grateful for, you may uncover some unpleasant memories and emotions. You can use this spell to put those to rest and heal. It will remind you that for us to have apples in abundance, nature had to turn dark the year before. So, to experience happiness again, you must go through some dark stages in your life.

You Will Need:

- 1 apple

- A knife

Instructions:

1. Cut the apple horizontally, and place the halves on your altar. The center reveals the ancient pagan protection symbol, the pentagram.

2. As you look at the pentagram, try to visualize your grievances or areas of life that are out of balance. This can be a health issue you are going through or a mental or emotional issue.

3. Having identified the source of negativity, take the seeds out of the apple. You may need to cut the entire center out to remove all the seeds.

4. Once the seeds are removed, take both apple halves into your hands, and look at their center again. Envision a sphere of light in it and feel this light entering your hands.

5. Now take the seeds and bury them underground. If you have a large enough backyard, you can plant the seeds there so they can grow into a tree. If the space is tight, you can place them in a small pot and consider the planting symbolic.

6. Say the following when you are planting the seeds:

   "With the healing energy of this apple, I nourish my mind, body, and soul. As the earth nourishes these seeds, taking my worries away, so shall nature nourish me by healing me and making me stronger."

7. As you are about to cover the seeds with soil, focus on feeling your negative emotions and thoughts disappear.

8. After the seeds are planted, wash your hands, and eat the apple while sensing its healing energy coursing through your body and soul.

Releasing Spell

The falling autumn leaves are the perfect ingredient for a releasing spell. Besides all the other significances, Mabon is also the time for letting go. As the leaves fall from the trees to the ground, they symbolize things weighing you down. You can lift this burden from your shoulders by simply using these leaves in a Mabon spell.

You Will Need:

- A bunch of leaves of different colors, shapes, and sizes

- A marker

Instructions:

1. Gather the leaves in a bowl and place them on your altar. You can put them on a table too, but an altar can help you set your intention better.

2. Take a leaf and focus on something you want to release from your life. Write a word or short phrase representing whatever you want to let go of.

3. When you are ready to let go, take the leaf into your hands and recite the following spell:

"With this leaf, I release my attachment to anything that does not align with my values.

I'm letting go of [what you have written on the leaf] and all the hurt it caused."

4. Repeat the process on a different leaf and feeling, setting your intention for letting go of each individual sentiment. Repeat until you run out of things you want to release.

5. Place each marked leaf back into the bowl and take it outside.

6. Release them one by one, letting the wind carry them away, along with your hurt.

7. As the negativity makes its way out from your body, you will feel it leaving more room for positive, healing energy.

Mabon Bath

The abrupt temperature changes brought on by the approaching winter can take a toll on your body and spirit. You will need a hot bath to warm you from the inside out. Taking a bath on the eve of the fall equinox is another great way to celebrate Mabon. A hot bath can be a tool for spiritual opening, healing from past trauma, or protection against the effects of the upcoming cold and dark period.

You Will Need:

- 1/3 cup of sea salt
- 1/3 cup of powdered milk or milk substitute
- 1/3 cup of oatmeal
- 1 teaspoon of dried calendula flowers
- 1 teaspoon of dried chamomile flowers
- 5-10 drops of myrrh essential oil
- 5-10 drops of frankincense essential oil
- Several candles, white and autumn-colored ones
- The incense of your choice (optional)

Instructions:

1. Scoop the oatmeal into a blender or food processor and blend until it reaches the consistency of flour. Pour it out in a separate bowl.

2. Mix the sea salt with the powdered milk or substitute in another bowl, and slowly mix in the dried flowers.

3. Now add the oatmeal and make sure that it coats the rest of the ingredients.

4. Add the essential oil and mix until well combined. You can add less or even a little more if the number of drops in the recipe does not get you the desired fragrance strength.

5. Fill your bathtub with warm water and add the mixture to it.

6. While you are waiting for the mixture to dissolve, decorate the edges of your tub with candles.

7. If you are using incense, light them up. You can skip this step if you find the scent of dissolving flowers relaxing enough.

8. Get into the bath, close your eyes, and meditate on whatever you wish to come to terms with for 30 minutes. You can also ask your spiritual guides for protection by focusing your intention in that direction.

Mabon Balance Spell

While a balancing spell can be performed at any time, its potency around an equinox is magnified. During this time, nature's dark and light sides are in balance, but not for a long time. With the fall equinox, the balance soon shifts towards the dark side, only to shift back toward the light one at the spring equinox. With this spell, you can celebrate this balance, empower it, and make the shift even more beneficial for you.

You Will Need:

- An 11-inch-long white ribbon
- An 11-inch-long black ribbon
- A white pencil or marker
- A black pencil or marker
- A charm or an object that symbolizes balance in your life
- 1 black candle
- 1 white candle
- Incense of your choice
- Acorns, nuts, leaves, and other harvest symbols
- Pieces of cloth or craft material in colors associated with Mabon

Instructions:

1. Before you cast the spell, search out areas in your life that you want to balance. Keep in mind that you should look for polar opposites. For each problematic area, the opposite is the solution.

2. The trick is to take the quality you find problematic and channel it in a different direction to balance out its past effects. Having done that, you will be ready to re-establish the balance.

3. Sit at your altar and place all your tools on it. Light the candles and the incense and arrange the rest of the items around them.

4. Take the black ribbon and the white marker or pencil and write down the quality you feel that you have in excess.

5. Then take the white ribbon and the black marker, and write the quality you lack or of which you need more in your life.

6. Line the ribbons on top of each other and tie them together at one end by leaving an inch off. While you do this, recite the following spell:

    "As winter is to summer, as dark is to light,

    As a god to a goddess, as the day is tonight,

    Let me find the perfect balance within me

    So, I may live in harmony."

7. Tie another knot an inch below the previous one and repeat the spell. Continue this until you have eight knots on the ribbons.

8. Tie the other end of the ribbon around the object that symbolizes balance for you and say:

    "By the ancient powers of three times three,

    this balance is my will, so let it be!"

9. You have successfully created a charm that you can take anywhere around Mabon, so you will always have a reminder of the power of this holiday.

10. Carry the charm close to your body until you gain the balance you were looking for.

Second Harvest Gratitude Spell

As the second harvest is in the middle of the fall season, we have plenty to be grateful for. If you have a garden or a field full of crops, you will be preparing to harvest your bounty or have just done so. And if you do not grow your own produce, getting close to the transition from the third quarter of the year can remind you of everything else you have achieved (harvested spiritually) throughout the year. Putting away your bounty fills you with relief, but it can also be a bittersweet experience as you know that nature is about to die. This spell can help you express your gratitude for your bounty as you are putting it away.

You Will Need:

- A black candle

- Dried sage

- The carrier oil of your choice

Instructions:

1. Place your tools on the altar and mix the sage with the oil.

2. Anoint your candle with the oil herb mixture and light it.

3. As you gaze into the candle flame, visualize yourself putting your tools down as you prepare to rest after a productive harvest season.

4. Take a deep breath and recite the following spell:

    "The harvest is over, so I can allow myself

    to rest and relax.

    I am thankful for all I have gathered

    as I prepare for the next season."

5. Let the satisfaction of a productive year fill you as you send out gratitude to all your guides and nature itself.

A Charm for Finding Peace

Albeit magical, the fall season is a stark reminder that winter is just around the corner, something many of us have trouble coming to terms with. Not to mention how stressful preparing for the Mabon festivities can be, especially when planning a large family gathering or community event. This charm can help you find peace, so you can enjoy the festivities and await the winter without stressing out or worrying about anything going wrong.

You Will Need:

- 1 small rose quartz
- 1 small hepatite stone
- 1 teaspoon of dried calendula
- 1 teaspoon of crushed sunflower seeds
- 1 teaspoon of sage
- 1 teaspoon of lavender
- A small white bag made of cloth

Instructions:

1. Put all of the above ingredients into the bag and close it.

2. Charge the charm you have just created with the following spell:

   "Surging waves of peace

   Wash over me, envelop me fully

   So, I can relax and feel the calm fill me

   So, I can relax and enjoy this time fully."

3. Take the charm with you everywhere you go. When you feel stressed out, just take the charm into your hands and let its magic permeate your soul.

4. Repeat the spell once again in your head if you are in the company of others or out loud if you are alone.

Transition Spell

Unlike the previous ones, this spell is geared toward the transition from summer to autumn. It helps you accept that while the warm days are over, not everything is dark yet. It also allows you to pause mid-harvest, take a step back from your busy schedule and find the balance that will prepare you for the winter.

You Will Need:

- An open space full of greenery

- A packet of dried herbs

Instructions:

1. Go to a park or find any patch of nature around you. Take your packet of herbs with you.

2. If the weather is still warm enough, sit on the ground or bench. If it is too cold, just stand in one place for a few minutes.

3. Take the packet of herbs into your hands and take it into your environment. Observe every detail in nature, and appreciate the beauty that surrounds you. If there are other people around you, look at them as well.

4. The more you focus your attention on the little details, the more you feel the time slowing down. Now say the following:

   "As I take in the abundant gifts of nature's divinity,

   I sense the protection that covers us.

   Mabon comes with a precious balance,

   The second time of the year.

   Abundance still flows,

   and through our labor, our bounty grows.

   While winter's cold is coming soon.

   Mabon still brings hope and joy.

Challenging times are drawing near,

I am blessed with an abundance this year.

Mabon brings color to land and tree

As it dresses nature, preparing it for slumber.

As my spirit embraces the dwindling light,

So, I will be ready for the long and cold night."

5. Let go of your worries and judgments and embrace the balance that Mabon brings.

Autumn Blessing Spell

This simple blessing spell can give you peace of mind before you lay your head to rest as you prepare for the coming winter. It can be conducted for a few days leading to the equinox, and by the time Mabon night comes, you will receive the blessing you need for your spiritual balance.

You Will Need:

- 1 white candle
- 1 black candle

Instructions:

1. Place the candle at the side of your altar and decorate the space around them with leaves, grapes, and other fall fruits.

2. When you are ready, light the candles and say the following:

   "I light these candles to honor the harvest season

   and to acknowledge the abundance in my life.

   I strive to remember each blessing I have received

   and for which I haven't said thanks throughout the year.

   I now want to share these gifts with those around me

   and with those who are not as blessed as I am now.

   I am grateful for having my spiritual guides, and I thank them for all the gifts they have yet to give me this season."

3. Let the candles burn for a couple of minutes as your body and mind relax, then extinguish them and go to sleep.

Corn Dolly Spell

At the heart of the Mabon harvest lies gratitude and generosity. As they are made from parts of the crops harvested the previous fall, corn dollies are great tools for giving thanks for the bounty in your life. This spell will enable you to express your gratitude and share your harvested goods with others. You can perform it alone, but it will be even more potent if enacted by a group.

You Will Need:

- A corn dolly for every participant
- A bonfire or candle

Instructions:

1. If you want to enact the spell alone, sit at your altar and light a candle. If done as a group, you should start by building a bonfire and sitting around it.

2. Each participant should pass a corn dolly through the smoke of your fire source while reciting the following:

    "I ask this dolly to protect my home and those inside it.

    I ask it to keep any disaster, illness, or human malice away from us."

3. Upon finishing the chant, throw the corn dolly into the fire or remove it from your altar if you are casting the spell inside your home.

Spiritual Preparation Bath

Take this bath a week before Mabon and repeat it on the night of the equinox to cleanse your spirit and prepare it for the upcoming changes.

You Will Need:

- Red and purple candles
- A handful of sea salt
- 5-10 drops of jasmine oil
- 5-10 drops of apple blossom oil
- 1 teaspoon of dried calendula petals
- Seeds from one pomegranate

Instructions:

1. Place the candles around your bathtub and light them.
2. Draw warm water into the tub and pour in the rest of the ingredients.
3. Get in the tub and rest for at least 30 minutes.
4. While you soak, set your intention on accepting balance and asking for protection from your spiritual guide.

Chapter 10: Mabon Prayers and Blessings

This final chapter explains different types of prayers and blessings that can be read during meditation or to celebrate Mabon. It starts by highlighting the significance of this practice and also states the prayers for various pagans, particularly Wiccans and Druids. Finally, the chapter provides details that can help readers create or personalize their prayers and blessings according to their spiritual beliefs.

Significance of Mabon Prayers

Mabon is a time when pagans get the opportunity to reflect and celebrate the results of their hard work and patience. Pagan rituals are inspired by farming activities and are held when crops have been harvested. The celebrations are intended to give thanks to the gods and goddesses for bestowing blessings on families and communities through a solid supply of food during the colder winter months. This is also a time for sharing; those who were blessed with abundant food supplies share with the less fortunate.

Falling on the day that light and dark periods are equal, this is also the right time for individuals to focus on the god and goddess that are represented by the sun and moon, which are fundamental to the pagan belief system

You can choose any way that suits your belief system to celebrate Mabon. However, the focus should be on the balance between dark and light or the second harvest. The following are some of the few rituals you may want to try for your celebration of abundant gifts from the earth.

Modern Celebrations

Modern Druids still celebrate Mabon, but they name the celebration: Alban. It is also a celebration at a time when light and dark are equal. The Asatru groups use it to honor the fall of the equinox, while Neopaganism and Wiccans use the time for community and kinship activities. Depending on your spiritual beliefs, the following are some of the prayers you should know.

Abundance Prayer

Mabon is meant to acknowledge the bounty of harvests and share with the less privileged members of your society. When you celebrate Mabon, you should give thanks for everything you have. This is a time to focus on balance and harmony within your person and around you. It is a good time to be around family and friends and show gratitude.

It is good to be thankful for what you have, including food, health, or even material blessings. Take time to realize that not all people are fortunate. A prayer for what you are grateful for is appropriate here. The following is a simple prayer for Thanksgiving and showing gratitude for the things you have.

Prayer of Gratitude

"I am blessed with all in my life,

and cannot help but give thanks.

I have an abundance,

and am grateful for what I have been given.

Some are not as fortunate as I,

and I know this to be true.

So, I pray for them as I accept my blessings,

to those who watch over and protect me:

please shower others with what I have been given,

and bring blessed balance to all."

When you honor the god or goddess, remember to recite this prayer. You can also provide an offering of your choice.

Mabon Balance Prayer

The light and the dark are in perfect balance. This can affect people in many ways, where some use the time to honor the darker elements of the goddess. Because of the balance, people can be drawn in both directions, and this can make a soul restless.

This can be felt through indecision or a feeling of intuition that everything is not as it should be. You can meditate through this or offer prayers.

Mabon Prayer of Balance

"The light and dark are balanced,

and we give thanks to Mabon for this,

and to all the gods and goddesses for their blessings.

We cannot have the bad without the good.

And hope is only apparent when we feel despair.

And love is what conquers the pain.

And we cannot rise once more without falling first.

That is the harmony we seek,

and we pray for it to grow within us."

Mabon Prayer to the Vine

The Mabon season is also characterized by rich vegetation, more pronounced in vineyards. During this time, grapes are in full season, and they should be used to celebrate the deities linked to the vine's growth and winemaking. The god of the vine must be honored in harvest celebrations.

Use the following prayer when you conduct your Mabon celebrations. Feel free to include anything that makes it more personal to you. Remember to ask the gods for more blessings in your prayer. You can also use it to ask anything you want the gods to provide during the next season.

Prayer of the Vine

"Hark! Hark! Hark!

We have harvested the grapes!

Their blood has become our wine!

The barrels are filled to the brim!

Hail Dionysus! Hail Bacchus!

Come celebrate with us,

And give us your blessings!

Hark! Hark! Hark!"

Prayer to the Dark Mother

If you have a strong connection to the dark elements of the year, you can consider hosting a ritual to honor the Dark Mother. Use this time to honor the Dark Mother because even though she is the one who brings the darkness, we cannot have the light without her.

While many people associate darkness with evil or bad things, several positive aspects can be obtained from embracing the dark component of life. However, this should only be for a short time. Let us call upon those who bring the dark and give them a blessing at this time.

Prayer for the Dark Mother

"Day gives way to the night,

just as life gives way to death,

and we dance with the Dark Mother.

Hecate, Kali, Tiamet,

Nemesis, Demeter, Morrighan,

those who bring destruction so everything can be rebuilt,

I still give thanks even as the darkness comes,

and the world descends into that darkness."

Thanksgiving Prayer for Mabon

This is a time to recognize the blessings in your life and give thanks for what you have. What do you have that brings you joy? How has the world blessed you? How have you benefitted from the gods and goddesses? Think about all you have, big and small.

Mabon Prayer of Thanksgiving

"We have reaped when we have sown,

the ground becomes barren.

The animals have come home for the season.

But we are not short on blessings,

for our plates are full,

and we give thanks to the gods and goddesses."

Count Your Blessings

Mabon is a time for giving thanks for everything we have. In some instances, people may take their fortunes for granted, which is not a good thing to do. Take time to reflect on your fortunes and blessings. Create a gratitude list including all the things you are happy to have in your life. No matter how small or big the things you have, they should get equal recognition in your prayers. Keep your list in a place where you can access it easily to perform your simple rituals.

Home Protection Prayer

The goddess Morrighan will help to bring protection to your home and the land surrounding it. This can be in advance of any threats you might face or because you have felt unsafe in the place you live.

"Oh, Morrighan! Oh, Morrighan!

Protect this land from those who would trespass upon it!

Oh, Morrighan! Oh, Morrighan!

Protect my lands and all who live within!

Oh, Morrighan! Oh, Morrighan!

Keep an eye over my family and me!

Oh, Morrighan! Oh, Morrighan!

You know a good fight, so fight for me,

The welder of the shield and protector of all,

Please listen to my call.

Turn back all those who seek to trespass on my land,

Show them that you show no mercy to those with evil in their hearts.

Keep my land in your heart,

And repulse wrongdoers.

And show your wrath.

Oh, Morrighan! Oh, Morrighan!

We are thankful for your blessings!

Oh, Morrighan! Oh, Morrighan!"

Raise Some Energy

Apart from conducting a prayer for Mabon balance, there are also other rituals you can celebrate to raise energy. Working in groups with family and friends to celebrate Mabon will raise group energy, and one of the most effective ways to achieve this is to use drums, bells, rattles, and other instruments. Others without instruments can clap their hands.

Begin the ritual with a regular but slow rhythm and increase the tempo gradually. End the drumming and clapping at some pre-arranged signal, and you will begin to feel the energy flow in waves. Chanting accompanied by dance is another method that can be used to raise group energy.

Mabon Balance Meditation

Another way of raising your energy is to engage in Mabon Balance Meditation. When you have been feeling spiritually or emotionally low, you can use meditation to re-balance your energy. Start by finding a comfortable place to do your meditation. You want to choose a place where you will not be disturbed and where you will also have room to do the meditation.

You will need a black candle and a white candle for the meditation. Start by placing the candles in a secure place and lighting them in any order. Start to breathe—breathe in and out slowly, focusing on your breath. Shut your eyes, and start to see in your mind all the obstacles blocking the harmony and balance in your life. See what positive change would look like. Focus on the solutions to your problems.

See the negative in your life slipping away, being replaced by positive energy. You might see this as streams flowing to and from you. Take stock of your goals, your friendships, and the romance in your life, and be thankful for the good while drawing positive energy toward you. Know that there is hope, no matter how you might feel right now. When you finish meditating, you should remember all the lessons you have learned and apply them in the future.

Celebrate Home and Hearth

The colder months naturally draw us inside for longer periods. This is the perfect time to declutter your home, your life, and your energy. You can perform a smudging along with cleaning your home. Sweetgrass is traditional for smudging.

When you are building an altar or decorating your home during Mabon, remember to use what might have been harvested in ancient times. Use imagery of the harvest, both the crops and the tools. You can also use this opportunity to give away the things you no longer need. Make repairs to your home in preparation for the hearth celebrations.

Hold a Ritual of Gratitude

To begin this ritual, decorate your altar with appropriate seasonal symbols representing abundance. Some of the items you can consider for your altar include the following:

- A gold or green candle signifies abundance.

- Baskets of fruits such as grapes and apples since they are associated with harvest.

- Create Gratitude Oil to use for the ritual. You need five drops of rose oil, 1/8 cup base oil of your preferred choice, two drops of vetiver oil, a pinch of ground cinnamon, and one drop of agrimony oil.

- Colors associated with abundance, especially green and gold.

- Cornucopias symbolize the season's bounty.

- Craft an abundance mandala. You can paint one or create a piece of art with three dimensions.

- Photos of important people.

- Symbols of the items for which you are thankful.

Take time to reflect on the things you have in abundance. These are not only limited to financial or material possessions. A satisfactory career, loving family, and abundant friends are some of the things you can be thankful for. To begin the rite, use gratitude oil to anoint the candle and light it on your altar. Pray to the gods and goddesses that are more powerful at this time of the year, and offer thanks and gratitude for what is bountiful in your life.

The next step is moving around your altar, reciting the things for which you are happy and thankful. You must also state why you are thankful for something and ask God to continue blessing you. If you do not want to do this alone and prefer to have people around, you can all offer gratitude.

The act of gratitude can be as simple as saying out loud what you are thankful for or taking a minute to meditate on your gratitude. Think about the things, people, and energies you are thankful for. It is essential to understand that gratitude is a gift, so you should continue giving to needy people. Giving something to another person helps you realize that you are fortunate to have the things that someone does not have.

When you make your gratitude ritual, you may need to let the individuals who make you happy know about the occasion. This will also help them to appreciate you. If you wish to send your gratitude directly to someone, you should let them know your intentions. This will also help them appreciate you, which can increase your blessings. Being appreciated by many people means that you are likely to enjoy more gifts from the provider. Make sure you end your ritual by tidying up everything you have covered and ask the god or goddess to continue blessing you.

Decorate Your Mabon Altar

Setting up and decorating your Mabon Altar is a critical component recognized by many pagans. An altar is used for different purposes, such as worship or prayer, a sacred place where you can perform ceremonies, meditation, or cast spells. The altar must be decorated with items that symbolize abundance and should also have fire, water, earth, and air elements. You can also include other items like a goddess candle or anything representing the gods you worship. When you decorate your altar, you must be guided by your spirituality.

Many pagans use their altar to keep spells or ritual-casting tools they use regularly. Other people decorate their altars for specific seasons and ceremonies. For Mabon, the act of choosing colors like reds, yellows, browns, and oranges shows gratitude and thankfulness. You can also include other things that symbolize the harvest season, such as wheat, apples, corn, and seasonal vegetables.

Mabon celebrations are associated with thanking the god and goddess for the things you have in life. They are usually held during the time of the second harvest and are conducted to honor the providers for blessing you with the things you need in life. Most celebrations are accompanied by prayers and different rituals depending on your spiritual beliefs. Most pagans use various items that symbolize abundance in their celebrations. When you perform any ritual, remember to include everything you want and thank the gods and goddesses for what you already have.

Conclusion

Whether you look at it from a religious perspective or an astrological point of view, the time of the autumn equinox is when a lot of changes are taking place. For Wiccans, this time of the year has considerable importance and is celebrated as one of the most joyous occasions of the year. It is one of the eight Wiccan Sabbats celebrated throughout the year. Many people consider this time to be celebrated to show gratitude for a successful harvest. This is usually done by various rituals, ceremonies, and grand feasts.

You can try any of the delicious recipes provided in the chapters, but make sure to add at least one of the dishes to your menu, which features signature ingredients such as apples, pomegranates, turkey, or potatoes. Make the most of this event by planning some ritualistic and general family activities to give thanks to the deities for the harvest of the autumn equinox. Whether you try a bonfire, a picnic, or simple foraging, make sure that you go in groups to spend most of the time with your friends, family, and loved ones. While you are performing these activities, do not forget to count your blessings and celebrate the harvest's abundance by saying a few Mabon prayers and blessings.

Fill your Mabon festival with abundance spells and charms to manifest the power of the equinox into your spells. Other purification and cleansing spells will work best during this time. Make sure that you follow the step-by-step instructions provided in the book to cast the various spells and charms. Deviating from the steps could make the spells less effective and ruin your spellwork.

Mabon is a time of celebration, and as such, many crafts, decorations, activities, and rituals are performed to commemorate this joyous time. You can tell stories associated with Mabon or make delicious feasts filled with the book's savory and sweet Mabon dishes. Add the different blessing rituals to this mixture, and you have got the perfect Mabon festival.

Here's another book by Mari Silva that you might like

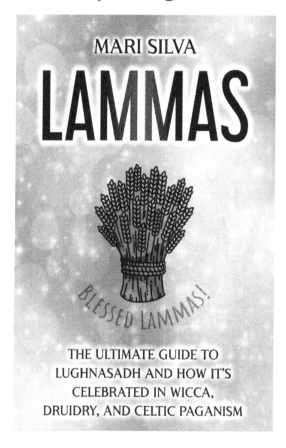

MARI SILVA

LAMMAS

BLESSED LAMMAS!

THE ULTIMATE GUIDE TO
LUGHNASADH AND HOW IT'S
CELEBRATED IN WICCA,
DRUIDRY, AND CELTIC PAGANISM

Your Free Gift (only available for a limited time)

Thanks for getting this book! If you want to learn more about various spirituality topics, then join Mari Silva's community and get a free guided meditation MP3 for awakening your third eye. This guided meditation mp3 is designed to open and strengthen ones third eye so you can experience a higher state of consciousness. Simply visit the link below the image to get started.

https://spiritualityspot.com/meditation

References

arithharger. (2017, September 18). The Autumn Equinox. Whispers of Yggdrasil. https://arithharger.wordpress.com/2017/09/18/the-autumn-equinox-2/comment-page-1/

Bhagat, D. (n.d.). The origins and practices of Mabon. Bpl.Org. https://www.bpl.org/blogs/post/the-origins-and-practices-of-mabon/

Crawford, C. (2020, September 15). What is Mabon, and how can we celebrate the Autumn Equinox? —. The Self-Care Emporium. https://theselfcareemporium.com/blog/what-is-mabon-autumn-equinox

Fall Equinox celebrations of Christianity, Pagans, Neopagans, etc. (n.d.-a). Religioustolerance.Org. https://www.religioustolerance.org/fall_equinox2.htm

Fall Equinox celebrations of Christianity, Pagans, Neopagans, etc. (n.d.-b). Religioustolerance.Org. https://www.religioustolerance.org/fall_equinox3.htm

Fall equinox rituals, herbs & recipes to celebrate mabon. (n.d.). Five Flavors Herbs. https://fiveflavorsherbs.com/blog/fall-equinox-rituals-herbs-recipes-to-celebrate-mabon/

Mabon house. (n.d.). Mabon House. https://www.mabonhouse.co/mabon

Mankey, J. (2014, September 16). The triumph of Mabon. Raise the Horns. https://www.patheos.com/blogs/panmankey/2014/09/the-triumph-of-mabon/

Mulhern, K. (n.d.). What are the sabbats. Patheos.Com. https://www.patheos.com/answers/what-are-the-sabbats

Rajchel, D. (2021). Mabon: Rituals, recipes & lore for the autumn equinox. Dreamscape Media.

Wigington, P. (2007, July 30). Mabon history: The second harvest. Learn Religions. https://www.learnreligions.com/mabon-history-the-second-harvest-2562060

Apel, T. (2020, August 16). Bacchus. Mythopedia. https://mythopedia.com/topics/bacchus

Apel, T., & Kapach, A. (2020, August 16). Hermes. Mythopedia. https://mythopedia.com/topics/hermes

Bhagat, D. (n.d.). The origins and practices of Mabon. Bpl.Org https://www.bpl.org/blogs/post/the-origins-and-practices-of-mabon/

Celtic religion - The Celtic gods. (n.d.). In Encyclopedia Britannica.

Dionysus. (2014, September 19). Greek Gods & Goddesses. https://greekgodsandgoddesses.net/gods/dionysus/

Dionysus. (2018, March 13). Greekmythology.Com; GreekMythology.com. https://www.greekmythology.com/Other_Gods/Dionysus/dionysus.html

Don't call me Mabon…. (2017, September 15). Hearth Witchery. https://annafranklinhearthwitch.wordpress.com/2017/09/15/dont-call-me-mabon/

Editors, C. R. (2018). Thoth: The history and legacy of the ancient Egyptian god who maintains the universe. Createspace Independent Publishing Platform.

Harter, N. (2005, September 1). Mabon: Journeying with Persephone. Llewellyn Worldwide. https://www.llewellyn.com/journal/article/893

heartofthewitchspath. (2016, August 11). ABCs of Celtic mythology – Mabon and Modron. Heart of the Witch's Path. https://heartofthewitchspath.wordpress.com/2016/08/11/abcs-of-celtic-mythology-mabon-and-modron/

Hermes. (2018, March 13). Greekmythology.Com; GreekMythology.com. https://www.greekmythology.com/Olympians/Hermes/hermes.html

Hermes and the Cattle of Apollo. (n.d.). Greek-Gods.Info. https://www.greek-gods.info/greek-gods/hermes/myths/hermes-apollo/

Locatelli-Kournwsky, L. (2018). Persephone. Archaia Studios Press.

Mabon: A pagan celebration. (2020, September 27). The Meredith Herald. https://www.meredithherald.com/post/mabon-a-pagan-celebration

Mabon ap Modron. (n.d.). Maryjones.Us. http://www.maryjones.us/jce/mabon.html

Maponos – mabon – Celtic god youth and hunting in Gaul and northern Britain. (n.d.). Celts & Myths.

https://celtsandmyths.tumblr.com/post/187395716920/maponos-mabon-celtic-god-youth-and-hunting-in

Me, A. (n.d.). Who is Mabon? Go Deeper http://www.godeeper.info/blog/who-is-mabon

Meehan, E. (2020, August 16). Thoth. Mythopedia. https://mythopedia.com/topics/thoth

No title. (n.d.). Study.Com. https://study.com/learn/lesson/egyptian-god-thoth-emerald-tablets-facts-quotes.html

O'Hara, K. (2022, May 21). The Morrigan: The story of the fiercest goddess in Irish myth. The Irish Road Trip. https://www.theirishroadtrip.com/the-morrigan/

The Morrigan: Crow goddess of death. (2015, June 20). Eternal Haunted Summer. https://eternalhauntedsummer.com/issues/summer-solstice-2015/the-morrigan-crow-goddess-of-death/

Worksheet Freelancer. (2019, July 23). Mabon facts, worksheets, history, symbols & traditions for kids. KidsKonnect. https://kidskonnect.com/holidays-seasons/mabon/

Wright, G. (2020, August 16). Cernunnos. Mythopedia. https://mythopedia.com/topics/cernunnos

(N.d.-a). Greekreporter.Com. https://greekreporter.com/2021/09/23/autumn-equinox-marks-solemn-change-of-seasons/

(N.d.-b). Theoi.Com. https://www.theoi.com/articles/what-is-the-demeter-and-persephone-story-summarized/

Caro, T. (2020, September 21). Magickal meaning & Symbolism of the pear tree. Magickal Spot. https://magickalspot.com/pear-tree-symbolism-meaning/

Greenhaven: A Pagan tradition. (n.d.). Greenhaven: A Pagan Tradition. http://greenhaventradition.weebly.com/mabon.html

Herbs sacred to mabon. (n.d.). Tripod.Com. https://cronescottage2002.tripod.com/thecottageaugustmabon2002/id10.html

The FruitGuys. (2021, September 2). Here's your fall fruit guide for 2019. The FruitGuys. https://fruitguys.com/2021/09/2021-fall-fruit-guide/

Wang, H. (2022, June 2). What fruit do you eat on the autumnal equinox? 8 recommended fruits for autumnal equinox. Sihai. https://en.4hw.com.cn/644/150862.html

Made in the USA
Coppell, TX
11 October 2022

84403978R00085